Art and Old Iron

*A Three Dimensional View of the
Industrial Revolution*

Models and
Photographs

by

Ron Jarvis

Beverley Books
Southwell
Portland

© Ronald Jarvis 2001

Published by Beverley Books
17 Sweet Hill Road
Southwell
Portland
Dorset DT5 2DS

All rights reserved. No part of this publication may be reproduced, stored in a retrieval system, or transmitted, in any form or by any means, electronic, mechanical, photocopying, recording or otherwise, without the prior permission of Beverley Books.

Typeset by **Dorchester Typesetting Group Ltd**
Printed by **The Friary Press**, Dorchester

British Library Cataloguing in publication Data

A Catalogue record for this book is available from the British Library

ISBN 0 9540688 0 7

CONTENTS

Contents	*iii*
Dedication	*iv*
Foreword	*v*
Men, Models and Machines	1
A Steam driven Water Wheel	4
Portable Power	13
Hypocycloidal Engine	19
The Small Engine	27
Sugar and Steam	33
Paddles against Propellers	38
The Horseless Carriage	46
Musket Barrels into Boilers	53
A Phantasmagorian	61
A Foretaste of the Future	69
The Gas Engine	77
The First Electric Train	84
Making the Models	95

Dedication

This book owes its existence to my dear wife
EVELYN

It was she who coped with a model maker who was always busily occupied when lunch was put on the table; it was she who understood and forgave when some very essential kitchen utensil disappeared, only to reappear as a sprocket or a clack or a grommet; it was she who cast oil on troubled waters when all things went wrong; and it was she who rejoiced and was glad when all went well.

Sadly, she passed away before the book was published but there remains a memory of her in every bit of every model and in every word of the book

Acknowledgements

Writing this book has been a venture in to the unknown for me: it would never have happened but for the prompting and continuous support of Denis Silverwood.

Help and encouragement in the building of the models over a period of nearly thirty years has come from a multitude of friends, and especially from Cherry Hill and from Alex Skinner.

Foreword

by

CHERRY HILL

This engaging book is about inventors of machines, their stories and achievements, and it is for those of us interested in industrial history and in men of history, as well as model engineers and ordinary people.

We are shown the inventiveness and spirit of the early Mechanics and we are reminded of the available equipment and conditions under which they lived and worked. The book takes us inside the minds of the inventors and the clear thinking necessary to build machines to do the job for which they were intended.

The long years of early steam development are covered very smoothly and clearly. I learnt much that I had not known before.

It is in the chapters on steam traction that we realise the unique designs and technical innovations required – albeit sometimes unsuccessfully – to overcome the hazards of travelling on the roads. I was particularly drawn to those chapters.

There is a long section on Dr Church's Phantasmagorian – a most involved engine and drive system. However, all the Steam Carriages chosen as prototypes are their own character; each the brain child of an inventor, whose name, sadly, is unknown to most people.

The section on Robert Davidson's electric train must be new to the majority of us. There clearly has been much historical research and practical experimentation by the author to authenticate this interesting chapter.

Finally, there is a chapter on the making of the models. It describes a wide ranging group of techniques which clearly have produced the perfect result. We must remember that all the models described are working models, many of which I have been privileged to see in operation.

I wish the book were twice as long.

List of Illustrations

	Page
Real life sizes, Author and his models	viii
Drawing of Savery's mine pumping arrangement	5
Wrigley's mill under construction	6
Wrigley's water wheel	7
Leet and sluice gate	8
Boiler and carding machine	9
Two of Hargreaves' spinning machines	10
Smeaton's portable engine of 1765	12
Smeaton's tower, somewhere in Cornwall	14
Valves and plug rod	16
Cylinder and snift valve	17
Hypocycloidal engine	20
Cylinder, pump and condenser	21
Hypocycloidal engine, bark grinder end of engine	22
Cylinder and hypocycloidal gears	23
View from above showing mitre gears driving the mill	24
James Watt's Bell Crank engine	26
Flywheel and cylinder of Bell Crank engine	28
Boiler, air pump and reservoir	29
Furnace door and electric controls	30
Stokers at work	31
Looking down on the cylinder and air pump	32
Beam engine used to crush sugar cane	33
Sugar extraction in the West Indies	34
Jukes Coulson's sugar extraction rollers and engine	35
Cane crushing rollers and bucket	36
The sugar cane factory in the West Indies	37
Two views of paddle steamers under construction	39
Steam Packet Co's steamer Red Rover being built	40
The main crank shaft and top of the engine	41
One of the two cylinders with piston rod and yoke	42
Main frames of the engine	43
Two engines viewed from the cylinder end	44
Trevithick's Steam Carriage	46
Front view of Trevithick's Carriage	48

	Page
The huge wheels of Trevithick's Carriage	50
The fire box door at the rear of the carriage	51
A Model Family	52
Julius Griffith's horseless carriage	54
Front view of Griffith's carriage on some moorland road	55
The boiler and fire box at the rear end of the carriage	56
The grass hopper engine and copper condensers	57
Details of the engine from the Patent drawings	59
Doctor Church's Phantasmagorian	60
Side view of the Phantasmagorian	62
The steerable front wheel and the drivers seat	63
The guard in his look-out seat	64
The basic wooden framework	65
The flexible wooden wheel and pneumatic support	65
A view of the engines from the rear compartment	66
The copper dome removed from the turbo charger	67
The Phantasmagorian with half its skin remove	68
James Steam Drag	70
The covers removed from the Steam Drag	71
The fireman's seat and the boiler fire door	72
The steam Drag, viewed from underneath	73
With covers removed, showing the copper condenser	74
Three gas headlamps decorate James Steam Drag	75
Brown's Patent Specification of 1823	78
The decorated beam of Brown's Patent Gas Engine	79
The other part of Brown's Patent Specification	81
Samuel Brown's Gas Powered Water Wheel	83
Davidson's Electric Locomotive and carriage	85
Mackie's drawing of Davidson's electric vehicle	86
Davidson's poster, printed by electromagnetism	87
Mackie's drawing of Davidson's electric motor	88
Model of Davidson's electric motor	89
Model of Davidson's Electric Locomotive	90
Full size zinc – iron cell	93
Electrodes of the zinc – carbon cell	94

Real life sizes, the author and some of his models.

Chapter 1
MEN, MODELS and MACHINES

We are today at the beginning of a new way of life, when science and technology dominate almost every aspect of our lives. Today, we all take for granted scientific conceptions and methods which, only a few years ago, would have looked like black magic, and we make use of mechanical devices to enable us to perform superhuman tasks. The development of technology in recent years has been explosive and the effects on our lives equally so, but the origins of this revolution were modest indeed.

Two centuries ago, life followed the same even tenor that it had done since time immemorial. To most people this meant having to work from rise to set of sun to get sufficient to eat and to meet the demands of the favoured few to whom circumstances of birth had given domination ever them. The production of food then, as now, required mechanical power. In those days, this came in the form of animal or human muscle power, supplemented, where circumstances permitted, by natural energy obtained from windmill or watermill. But it was when it dawned on people that abundant energy could be obtained, cheaply, by harnessing the power of steam, where and when it was wanted, that the fantastic change which we now know as the Industrial Revolution began. It was a change that was to alter the lives of mankind the world over.

The people who sparked off the revolution fall, more or less, into two groups. There were the 'Natural Philosophers' – today we would call them 'Scientists' – and then there were the 'Inventors'. These latter were to become known as 'Mechanics' because they were concerned with machines; today they have acquired the title of 'Engineer', but in those days this was the special title of the soldiers whose duty it was to look after the engines of war, the cannon and the fortifications.

The first group of people, – the philosophers, were concerned with acquisition of knowledge about the mysterious ways of nature, and they cared less about the benefits which might accrue from it. Their curiosity laid down a firm knowledge of natural laws and their names are now enshrined in the history of science. Volta and Faraday, Boyle and Lavoisier, Carnot and Kelvin and so many others will forever be remembered for the natural laws and for the phenomena that they discovered. Their work, and their curiosity and their knowledge laid the foundations for a new way of living. However, it was left to more mundane people to build on those foundations. The inventors, by and large, were a different sort of folk. Unlike many of the philosophers, they had no great wealth or title or rank; often they had little more than the most rudimentary education. Their designation 'Mechanic' did not imply any special social standing such as did 'Doctor' or Parson'. To all intents and purposes, they were ordinary people with no claim to public attention; unnoticed in life, in death they were quickly forgotten. But they were the people who were able to bring the arcane pursuits of the academics out of the clouds and into real life. It is to them, more than to any other, that we owe the standard of life we enjoy today.

Not all these people have been forgotten, who has not heard of George Stephenson and his railway engine, the Rocket, or of Brunel and his bridges, of Watts, Newcomen and a dozen others? But so many have lived and died unsung.

Perhaps this little book will remind us of just a few of those forgotten geniuses and go some way to give a small credit where so much is due. Because little or nothing remains today of the original ironmongery, we have to rely on the drawings, written descriptions, and such other little bits of information that have survived the years, to get any idea of what the machines really looked like or how they actually worked in practice.

How wonderful it would be if we could unearth, from some remote place, the actual machines that started the industrial revolution. But this will never be. Today, we are just beginning to realise that these objects were, by right and in the truest sense of the word, 'ART' – worthy objects made by the hand of man. At the time of their conception, art played a very big part in the life of the educated and well-to-do people in this country. Artistic objects were valued and were preserved, so that they have survived and retained their value today. Not so the machines, they were generally considered to be anti-social and were often deliberately destroyed. They were little more than old iron. It is interesting today to consider what might be, for example, the selling price of Savery's original steam engine, supposing that it could be found, miraculously preserved, in some forgotten mine shaft. Would it fetch the same price in an art dealer's auction room as a Venus di Milo or a La Gioconda? Of course not, yet this engine, indirectly, has contributed incomparably more to the wellbeing of mankind than any picture or sculpture has ever done.

This book is about a modest attempt to bring to life something that at least resembles a few of the long lost and little known machines. It has often been said "One picture is worth a thousand words"; perhaps the same ratio exists between a picture and a three dimensional object. This can be touched, viewed from all angles, even from inside. It can be made to behave like its prototype and, in its making often brings to light lost details.

When I reached retirement age, as an electrical engineer, more than twenty years ago, I looked around for a hobby, which did not involve the complexity and the inaccessibility of modern electronics. I was drawn to the simplicity and to the beauty of the first simple steam engines, built in the years between 1760 and 1840. Since then I have constructed more than a dozen of them, not in full size, that would have been impracticable, but at a scale of one inch to the foot. They are all machines that have never "hit the headlines" but were unique or unusual even in their own time. The models, or at least their colour photographs, serve to give a far better picture of what the machines actually looked like in their heyday, than any contemporary artist's impression or written description could do.

Information about the machines has had to be gathered from a very wide range of sources; letters and reports, contemporary newspaper articles and the like. As interest in engineering grew, at the beginning of the 19th century, a technical magazine came on the scene. In 1817 the "Mechanics Magazine" appeared, coming out weekly at the price of 3 pence. It consisted mainly of letters from amateur scientists – gentlemen interested in almost any practical device or idea, from acupuncture to water closets. It also included many snippets of engineering news, many details of the machines then beginning to be developed, and so today it is one of the most valuable sources of information about the state of the art of engineering at that time.

The most authoritative information comes from the Patent Office. Petitions to the Sovereign for the sole right to use, exploit, or sell a new idea, began about 1700. At first, the granting of this right was rare, but as people began to realise the very considerable financial advantages of 'Patent rights', the number began to grow rapidly until by 1800 it had reached more than three thousand.

The importance was soon realised of making the essence of the idea clear and unequivocal, and so the Patent Specification evolved. As time went by, lawyers became more and more involved in the preparation of the document, but, especially in the early ones, the description of the machine had to be entirely the work of the inventor, a man usually more at home with a hammer and chisel than with a pen or brush. Mechanical drawing as we know it today had not yet evolved and so the Specification drawings range from very generalised diagrams to artistic productions. I was delighted, for example, to come across a very formal drawing of a beautiful steam locomotive and to find that the draughtsman had added some artistic and accurate drawings of the driver and fireman. They were seen from the front, from the side, and even in plan, looking down onto the driver's stovepipe hat. A Doctor who became an Inventor had made this particular drawing; it was beautifully drawn and the written descriptions were precise and clear, but it was very much an exception to the rule. Most Patent Specifications tended to be vague, most inventors wanted their Patents to cover as much ground as possible and so minor mechanical details were generally not included.

I soon found another problem associated with the information given by the original Patent descriptions. The Patent application was often made before the prototype machine had been built; usually by the time this had been done, the inventor had added new ideas or made alterations so that the real-life machine could have been very different from its initial conception.

Consequently, in presenting the models as illustrations of the original machines, I am only too well aware that they may contain some details that may not have been in the original. Nevertheless, each model is the culmination of a good deal of research and I am confident that, in general, they are good copies of their prototypes.

Although the models are only quite small, I have tried, in most of the photographs to disguise their actual size by putting false backgrounds that suggest that they are full size. The fact that the models are so much smaller than the machines that they are trying to simulate, brings many problems when it comes to making them work like their big brothers. Spinoza wrote, in 1660, "Nature cannot be scaled", and it is true that, as the size of the model is reduced, the natural forces acting within it do not scale down in proportion to its size. In extreme cases it may well be that a small model can never work in the same fashion as its full size counterpart. This was a problem that I had to meet by making changes where they could not be seen, usually to the works inside the machines. Where this was not possible, a difficult balance had then to be struck between a model which looked right and one which worked right.

Chapter 2

A STEAM DRIVEN WATERWHEEL

In about 1770, James Hargreaves invented a spinning engine called the Spinning Jenny; not a very breath-taking event it would seem. Nevertheless this simple piece of mechanism is now regarded as the first of a long chain of similar inventions which gave rise to the Industrial Revolution. In a primitive society, the first requirement of life is food, and in all but the hottest parts of the world, the next is protection from the weather, from the wind, and from the rain. Our earliest ancestors used the skin and fur of animals but, as the population grew, demand exceeded supply and other materials had to be found. Someone, somewhere, had the idea of taking vegetable and animal fibres, first twisting them into thin cords or threads, and then weaving the threads together to form a sheet. So an alternative to animal skins was found. Over a long period of time, the twin skills of spinning and weaving, slowly developed, together with the simple tools needed for the job.

Spinning must originally have been done by taking a small bunch of fibres, or perhaps wool, and twisting it between thumb and finger, continuously adding more and more to extend the thread. Perhaps, the thread might have been wound on to a piece of wood and so the whorl would have evolved. Much later on, a spindle that could be rotated by a larger driving wheel and an endless belt replaced the whorl. So the spinning wheel was invented and spinning became, in Europe at least, one of the essential skills required of every housewife. It would seem too, from our childhood fairytale books, of even the highest ladies in the land. The Princess, in her ivory tower, seemed to have nothing to do all day but to sing songs to her spinning wheel.

So, from time out of mind, thread was spun one thread at a time, a long and tedious process. Even the Princess, with all the time in the world on her hands must have found it a slow business to spin sufficient thread for even the scantiest of her garments. Then a man named Hargreaves invented the spinning machine and, alas, put an end to the maiden and her spinning wheel. His machine had none of its glamour but it did have the great advantage of spinning sixteen threads simultaneously. However, there was a price to be paid; it demanded, not only skill and dexterity, but also a considerable amount of muscular power – unlikely to be part of the make up of a fairy princess!

This fact was well recognised by Richard Arkwright. He was a barber and wig-maker, who, shortly after Hargreave had demonstrated his Spinning Jenny, had also invented a spinning machine. His version did not require the skill that Hargreaves' did, but it demanded more power than the human operator could provide. The time was ripe for the age-old skill of spinning to be taken over by a machine driven by something more powerful than a man or a woman. Arkwright's machine, which he first tried out in Nottingham in 1770, was powered by horses. This prompted him to build a mill at Cromford in Derbyshire where he installed a number of his spinning machines. It was the beginning of a new era. Soon, hundreds of his machines were working at Cromford and elsewhere – but they were not driven by horses.

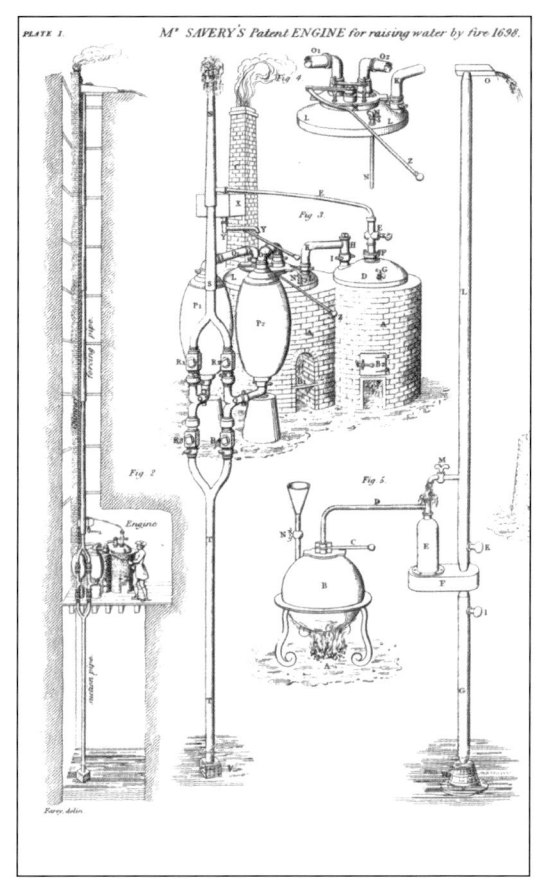

This was at a time when the steam engine, as we know it today, had not been dreamed of. It is true that, in Roman times, Hero of Alexandria had made a toy in which steam, issuing from a pair of jets in a heated hollow container, caused the container to rotate. However it is unlikely that even the most learned of philosophers of Arkwright's day – had he even known of Hero's toy – would have associated steam with a rotary machine having power so much greater than that of a man. Yet this is just what a man named Wrigley succeeded in doing.

To see how his arrangement worked, it is necessary to go back to the early 1700's when Captain Thomas Savery devised a contrivance to pump water from flooded tin mines.

He described it in a book, published in 1702, which had the intriguing title of "The Miner's Friend, or an Engine to raise Water by Fire". The drawing opposite is taken from his book.

Fig. 5 of Savery's illustration shows how the arrangement works. B is a boiler that can be replenished with water, when required, through the funnel and tap N, and is connected to vessels E and F by a pipe and cock C. The vessel F has one pipe – the suction pipe – going down to the water in the bottom of the mine, and another going up to the top of the mine-shaft. This was the delivery pipe. Each pipe has a cock in it, adjacent to the vessels, and in addition there is a water tap in the delivery pipe that allows cooling water to be poured over the vessels. Operation of the machine depends upon the opening and closing of these cocks in the correct sequence and at exactly the right moment – a job entrusted to a small boy!

When steam had been raised, the boy made sure that cock I was closed and that cock K was open and then he opened the steam cock C. Steam filled the vessels E and F, driving any water in them out and up the delivery pipe L. He then closed the steam cock and also the cock K in the delivery pipe. Next, he turned on the water tap so that some of the water contained in the delivery pipe ran over the vessels, cooling and condensing the steam in them, thus creating a partial vacuum which, when he opened cock I, sucked up water from the mine. When he considered that the vessels were as full of water as they could be, he turned off cock I and then turned the steam cock on again, so recommencing the cycle all over again. Although he could not see inside the iron vessels, he could get a good idea of where the water level in them was, by the way the damp air of the mine condensed on the surfaces of the vessels. It must have been a hot and very uncomfortable job for a small child who would have had to keep his wits about him to be sure that he got everything turned on and off in the proper order.

Wrigley used Savery's method of pumping water but he found ways of doing the boy's job with a much more reliable operating mechanism. He pumped water, not to empty a flooded mine, but to run a special water mill to drive his machines.

Wrigley's Mill under construction.

Today we have no idea what his original building looked like, but we do have a diagrammatic sketch of the water wheel and boiler and of the operating arrangements.

Since these parts of the system could not operate unsupported, I had to provide an appropriate building of the sort which, in 1750, Wrigley might have used to set up his machines. It is made of Portland stone with a slate roof and a flagstone floor and it is based on local building practice. It is typical of the period, except in one respect. Windows in those days were generally small, so as to conserve heat in the winter, but this one has been fitted with 'weaver's windows' to give plenty of light for the workers inside. Since it did not need a stream to provide power, it could have been built anywhere in a town or in the countryside. It could well have been an addition to an existing building.

Finished model of Wrigley's Steam Waterwheel.

Behind the wall and under the wheel, is a deep cistern filled with water. The rectangular box above is the leet from which water comes to turn the wheel. The water enters the leet, through a flap valve, from the black cylinder behind it. It is pumped there, from the cistern below, by Wrigley's own arrangement of the device that Captain Thomas Savery had suggested in 1701.

The leet and sluice gate lever.

The black cylinder corresponds to Savery's vessels E and F in his drawing. The flow of water, and so the speed of the wheel, is controlled by the lever on the front of the leet.

Attached to the axle of the water wheel is a wooden disc with two sets of wooden teeth projecting from the rim. As the wheel revolves, one of the teeth is caught up with the end of a pump handle, raising it and then allowing it to fall smartly, four times for each revolution of the water wheel. Each time the pump handle falls, it sends a jet of water up through a small pipe into the vessel, condensing the steam in it and creating a partial vacuum which sucks further water up into the vessel. Between each operation of the pump, one of the other teeth, momentarily opens a valve that sends a blast of steam into the vessel, expelling the water into the leet and refilling the vessel with steam.

Inside view of boiler and a carding machine.

Two Hargreaves spinning machines and a carding machine.

So long as steam was available to pump the water, the wheel would keep turning, using the same water over and over again. If the volume of the water was not large, it would soon become quite hot. What a sight it must have been! The wheel turning as if by magic, covered by a mist of white vapour and by clouds of black smoke from the chimney. No wonder that ordinary country folk thought that this was the work of the Devil.

Although Savery had used this method of pumping water from mines some 40 years earlier, other inventors had, in the interim, built more effective and efficient machines. Thomas Newcomen, using Spinosa's principle that "Nature abhors a vacuum" had built pumping engines – or, in the vernacular of the times, "Fire Engines" – in which, instead of using the vacuum to act directly upon the water to suck it out from the mine, he used it to pull upon a piston in a cylinder. The piston was connected to a mechanical pump at the bottom of the mine-shaft. James Watt had gone a step further and arranged the piston to be powered, not only by suction, but by the steam pressure as well. Motion of the piston was converted into rotary motion by means of a beam and crank. Both he and Wrigley were now able to offer machines that converted fire, through steam, into rotary motion.

James Watt's first machines gave a somewhat irregular rotation, but that of Wrigley was a smooth, easily controlled motion. It was much more suitable for the purpose of driving Arkwright's spinning machines. On the other hand, Watt's engines used much less coal to do the same amount of work. This was a factor that carried much weight with the hard-headed business men who ran the mills. Throughout Wrigley's life there was competition and, on Watts part, somewhat arrogant antagonism between the two inventors, but in the end it was the greater economy of James Watt's engines which counted most and Wrigley was forgotten.

The model of Wrigley's water wheel, is based upon a description given by John Farey, one of the first of a number of self-styled experts, the Patent Agents. He gives detailed information about the machine itself, but little about its surroundings, the buildings and the spinning machines. The Science Museum in London, has on show some of Arkwright's original machines and the author was privileged to be allowed to examine them in detail so that the pair of 8 spindle, spinning machines and the carding machine are truly representative of the sort of machines that Wrigley's steam waterwheel would have worked two hundred and fifty years ago.

The boiler is known as the "wagon" type; shaped rather like the old covered wagons that played so large a part in the development of the American West. The original boiler could well have been built of copper plates, and the top might have been no more than a sheet of lead, since the internal steam pressure would have been little more than atmospheric pressure. The hot gases from the fire in the grate underneath the boiler, circulated in flues in the brickwork surrounding it and then, through a damper, into the chimney.

Inside the boiler was a float, connected by means of a chain passing through a hole in the top of the boiler, to what looks like a w.c.cistern, fixed high on the wall near to the leet, from which it was filled with water. When the level of the water in the boiler fell, the chain was pulled down, allowing water from the cistern to flow through a small pipe back into the boiler to refill it again. The 'float' was made of stone! – it floated because its weight was partly balanced by the weight of the chain.

Coming as it did so early in the development of the machine, the whole system was a wonderful example of automatic control. In principle, at least, all that the engineer had to do was to put coal on the fire and to control the speed of the machine by opening or closing the sluice gate. Water, evaporated by the boiler was re-condensed in the vessel and, passing out with the main stream, was replaced into the system via the cistern. The valves that controlled the sequence of operations of the water wheel were either, self acting, or were opened and closed by the motion of the machine. It must be one of the earliest examples of the automatic control. It also pointed the way in which the Industrial Revolution would replace human effort in the factory and work-place with the power of steam.

Smeaton's Portable Engine, 1765.

Chapter 3

PORTABLE POWER

Joshua Wrigley's water wheel, although it obtained power from a boiler and the use of steam, was far removed from what is now our general idea of a steam engine. At least, however, it did succeed in making the "wheels go round". The first real steam engines did not go round, their job was to pump water and they simply pulled a glorified pump handle – the "Beam" – up and down. One end of the beam had a rod attached to it that extended down to the bottom of the mine and operated the actual pump; the other end was connected to a piston, pushed up and down in a cylinder by the power of steam. The action was slow and deliberate, large quantities of water had to be lifted with each stroke and in consequence, the whole machine had to be strong and heavy with massive wooden or cast iron beams and with equally sturdy buildings to support them. The many that remain today, in Cornwall and elsewhere, testify to the strength and permanence of the Cornish Beam Engine.

Unfortunately, the mines themselves were not so permanent. When the tin lodes ran out, the mine was closed, but the cost of dismantling the beam engine was often so great that it was more economical to leave it to rust away and to build afresh elsewhere. One builder of steam engines, John Smeaton, in 1765 recognised the need for engines that could be moved easily to a new site when their work was done at the old one.

Smeaton was a remarkable man, better remembered today, not for the steam engines he designed and built, but for his epic battle with the sea. He succeeded, where other previous attempts had ignominiously failed, in building a lighthouse on rocks exposed to all the fury of the wind and sea – the Eddystone Light. Today, an architect faced with such a task, would begin by calculating wind forces, foundation stability and a thousand other details before starting on the project. Smeaton simply used his inherent ingenuity and his knowledge of the materials he was working with to shape and dove-tail the building blocks of his tower in the sea. Many years later, it was dismantled and removed to Plymouth Hoe where it now stands as a tribute to his genius.

In their general design, most of his steam engines followed the accepted practice of his day; it was in all the smaller details, which he examined and tested both in theory and experimentally, that his machines excelled. However, his "Portable Engine" as he called it, was an exception to the general rule.

Standing some 30 feet high, the tall latticed wooden structure, surmounted by a wooden lead-lined water tank and flanked by the iron boiler with its chimney, had an elegance and a sense of suitability and aptness which matched the essentially practical but also graceful form of the Eddystone Lighthouse.

Smeaton's machine in operation developed about one horsepower. The cylinder is longer, and its bore is smaller than was customary at the time. Its designer thought that this would result in a more efficient engine, although subsequent experience

Smeaton's engine and tower as it might have looked, standing isolated over a tin mine somewhere in Cornwall

proved him wrong. The long stroke would ordinarily have required a very long beam with all the corresponding problems of extra weight and strength. He neatly avoided these difficulties by replacing the beam with a stout wooden wheel, able to rotate through a much greater arc than a beam could. A strong chain, passing round the wheel, connected the piston in its cylinder on one side of the machine with the pump rod hanging down the pit shaft on the other side.

The engine, although so different in structure from Wrigley's water wheel, nevertheless employed the same fundamental principle of operation; both are atmospheric engines. In each, steam is condensed inside a closed vessel, creating a partial vacuum in it that is used to suck up water from the mine-shaft.

In Smeaton's engine – as in all the early mine pumping engines – at an appropriate moment a valve is opened allowing steam from the boiler to flow into the vertical cylinder. This takes place as the piston is being drawn upwards by the greater weight of the pump rod hanging from the other side of the wheel. As the piston approaches the top of the cylinder the valve is closed, sealing off the cylinder; next, the water valve is opened, allowing a fine spray of cold water from the water tank placed at the top of the wooden support structure, to enter the cylinder. This results in a rapid condensation of the steam inside the cylinder and the consequent partial vacuum allows atmospheric pressure to force the piston downwards whilst the chain pulls up the pump rod on the opposite side of the wheel. This is the power stroke of the machine when the pump forces water up and out of the mine.

When the piston gets to the bottom of the cylinder, the steam valve is reopened and the cycle is repeated as the piston starts to rise, drawing in steam again. The two valves are opened and closed by the action of the 'Plug Rod', a heavy wooden rod hanging from a chain attached to the periphery of a smaller wheel secured to the main wheel. The plug rod, the pump rod, and piston thus operate in unison although the plug rod's movement is much less. It has a number of holes drilled into it, in which pegs may be set to trigger and then reset the valves, so determining the moment of operation of the valves as the pump rod goes up and down. The way the machine works is deceptively simple; in practice however there are complications that make the movements far from being easy to control.

The first problem is to get rid of the cooling water that is sprayed into the cylinder at each operation. Unless this is done, within a few strokes of the piston there would be sufficient water accumulated to stop all action. So a self-acting valve, called the "Horse foot clack" because of its similarity to a horse's hoof, is fitted to the bottom of the cylinder inside a closed trough leading back to the boiler. As steam is admitted into the cylinder, the rising pressure allows the water to flow out into the trough under the cylinder. The heat contained in this condensate has to be conserved in the interest of economy, so the hot water cannot be allowed to go to waste but has to be fed back , through a special non-return valve, into the boiler against the steam pressure. If this arrangement is to work, the steam pressure must not be allowed to rise more than the equivalent of a column of water equal to the height between the water in the boiler and that in the trough. In Smeaton's full size engine this was about 3 feet. In the model it is only 3 inches so that its boiler pressure must not exceed much more than about one tenth of a pound per square inch and the horse foot valve has to respond to a fraction of this.

Experience with the small scale model has shown how extremely critical the proper functioning of this valve is; particularly so, because the difficulty is aggravated by its small size and its inaccessibility. Eventually, an entirely new form of self-acting valve had to be devised before the model would work properly. One can well imagine what trouble Smeaton and his workmen must have had with this valve, situated as it was in an inaccessible closed box placed underneath the hot cylinder.

Yet another problem was the 'Snift clack'. This got its name because, when in operation, it made a noise like a man blowing his nose! Its job was to get rid of the air which, initially dissolved in the feed water in the boiler, also accumulated in the cylinder. This valve, a flap valve hanging at the base of the cylinder, was at least much more accessible than the horse foot valve, but it had to be adjusted with great delicacy.

The model had its own peculiar difficulties of disproportionate heat transfer and losses. It was found necessary to line the cylinder with PTFE to prevent heat loss there. These problems would also have affected Smeaton's machine, but to a lesser extent than in the model, and it seems that he recognized some of them. For example, he used wooden pipes for the cooling water to prevent it being heated by the warm parts of the machine.

Smeaton was the one of the first of the Mechanics to look at the machines of his day with what we might call the eye of an experimental scientist and he laid down rules whereby the efficiency of a pumping engine might be measured. He compared engines one with another and discovered their failings, where the faults lay, and what could be done to improve them. He built a small experimental engine, similar to this, which he installed in his own house and upon which he carried out all manner of experiments – it was a test bed on which to try out his ideas. The Portable Engine stands out because it so different from its contemporaries; it is a true masterpiece.

There is another way in which this machine shows a change of thinking; the very concept of portable machines was something quite new. Buildings then were built to last for ever, this was a massive structure which its designer intended should be taken apart when its job was done. Just as Smeaton devised ways of joining his stone blocks for the Eddystone lighthouse so they should never be broken, equally cleverly he designed all the beams and struts so that they could come apart and be reassembled. Was this the beginning of Meccano!

But like all the other wonderful machines, this one has disappeared for ever. What a wonderful companion it would make to Smeatons other masterpiece if we could have both of them standing beside each other on Plymouth Hoe.

It is so easy today, with our wealth of technical expertise, to smile at these crude machines and their makers. It is only when the machines are actually made to work that some of their hidden complexities come to light, and it is only now when modern techniques are able to demonstrate some of the ways in which those Mechanics of old found answers to the problems, that we can appreciate their cleverness and ability. The simple and often inaccurate drawings and descriptions that have come down to us from so long ago disguise the ingenuity and intellectual power of those 'simple' people.

Chapter 4

THE HYPOCYCLOIDAL ENGINE

At the time when Joshua Wrigley was building his steam water wheels, other brains were at work devising more simple mechanical means of converting the irregular movement of a piston in a cylinder into a regular rotary motion. Smeaton's arrangement did this but it was bulky and inconvenient. A more compact engine was wanted so that the power of steam could be easily used for industrial purposes.

In Edinburgh, another young inventor, James Watt, was taking a closer look both at the theory and at the practical way in which the atmospheric engine worked. His experiments showed that the use of a separate vessel, in which the exhaust steam from the engine was cooled and condensed, resulted in a great improvement in the efficiency of the machine. It was a big step forward in adapting the power of steam to the needs of industry but there still remained the mechanical problem of changing the up and down movement of the atmospheric mine pumping engine to the steady rotary motion needed in the factory or workshop.

It was not a new problem. Denys Papin, as early as 1670 had suggested that by putting several cylinders side by side, with each piston pushing a toothed rack against a separate ratchet wheel on a common shaft, it would be possible to obtain smooth rotary motion. Other ratchet arrangements were put forward but none of them were very successful. Of course, the foot treadle of the domestic spinning machine with its crank and pedal must, at this time, have been a very familiar device which effectively converted the up and down motion of the foot into the smooth rotation of a spinning wheel. However, this does not seem to have been taken very seriously by the early builders of the steam engine, perhaps this was because the movement of the piston was irregular and the length of stroke was uncertain.

In 1780, James Pickard, a button maker from Birmingham, had taken out a patent for "A Method of applying steam engines, commonly called fire engines, to the turning of wheels; whereby a rotative motion, or rotation around an axis, is performed". His patent was for a connecting rod, hinged at the end of the piston rod, and connected to an offset crank pin, at the end of a rotating shaft. – similar to the spinning machine. Atmospheric pressure would push the piston in one direction and a counter weight would pull it back again. He appreciated that there would be two dead spots – at top and bottom dead centres – so to get the connecting rod over these, he fitted a toothed wheel on the shaft, driving another wheel with half the number of teeth. This wheel carried a heavy weight on one side that, as the connecting rod arrived at top or bottom centre, by being out of balance, carried it across the dead spot. Basically, his patent was little more than an elaboration of the spinning wheel treadle and it is doubtful if his claim for originality would stand.

When James Watt heard of the patent, he claimed that Pickard had stolen the idea from him, and that he had learned of the idea from one of Watt's workman who at that time was building an experimental engine for him. Whatever the truth of the matter, Watts evidently decided that litigation was not worthwhile.

The very existence of Pickard's patent worried many other engine builders and in consequence, different ways were devised of providing smooth rotation, although one or two other engine builders took a chance, fitted a straight forward crank and connecting rod and, it would seem, got away with it! James Watt's own answer to the problem was by the use of the sun and planet gear for which he is well known.

One of the problems of the simple crank is that, except when the piston is at top or bottom centre, the crank and connecting rod apply a lateral force acting on the end of the piston rod. The rod has to be supported against this force. Slide rails provide this support in modern steam engines, but in 1780 this simple solution had not been adopted.

James White, an English mechanic, who had lived for some time in France, came up with an ingenious arrangement that solved the problem. In this, the end of the piston rod was constrained to move only in a straight line by the relative action of two gear wheels, one of which provided the required rotation. The geometric basis of White's arrangement is the theorem that any point on the periphery of a circle, rolling within another circle of twice its radius, moves in a straight line which passes through the centre of the larger circle. Napoleon Bonaparte was so impressed with the idea that he awarded the inventor a special medal in recognition of his genius.

In 1802, the firm of Fenton, Murray and Woods, of Leeds, was commissioned to devise and build a steam powered machine which would grind oak bark into the small pieces for use in the tanning of leather. They were a newly arrived firm, hoping to get a foot into the lucrative business of building steam engines. Matthew Murray, by trade a blacksmith from Newcastle upon Tyne, was the engineer and inventor of the firm. Although he had to use some of Watt's patents, he was anxious to avoid what he could of them.

Boulton and Watt were on terms of relatively friendly rivalry with Fenton, Murray and Wood who were making their own iron castings for their steam engines. They were acknowledged to be considerably better than the castings that Boulton and Watt were producing at their Soho works. It is said that James Watt made a friendly visit to his rival's works where Murray was induced to drink so much fine ale that Watts was able to glean much of the firm's trade secrets from him. Another of Watts schemes was for one of his own workmen to get a job with Fenton, Murray and Wood. Later he returned to his original masters, and passed on more of their secrets. One of these secrets was their practice of paying their workmen at 11 o'clock on Saturdays. This time enabled the wives of the men to come and collect their husband's wages before the latter could spend them in the local pub. Was this an example of industrial psychology or just an expression of moral rectitude ?

James White's geometric arrangement for obtaining rotary motion must have seemed ideal to Murray and so he set about converting theory into practice. The resulting machine with its compact vertical steam engine, combined with the oak bark mill – like an over-sized coffee mill – was indeed well suited to its purpose. It was entirely self contained. When in action its motion was intriguing and fascinating.

The picture below shows the machine from the steam engine end, and it shows how the hypocycloidal motion was arranged. The large circular ring, with teeth cut into the inner side, is mounted above the cylinder on an iron frame, supported by square fluted pillars, The frame also carries the main engine shaft and bearings, The axis of the main shaft passes through the centre of the large toothed ring. Attached to the end of the shaft is a stout disc with an offset stub axle on which the other wheel – the planet wheel – runs. Its teeth match those of the large ring but it has only half its number. An arm, attached to the planet wheel has, at its end, another stub axle to which the end of the piston rod is coupled. The axis of this stub axle is at the same radius as the pitch circle of the teeth of the planet wheel. So, as the main shaft goes round it carries with it the planet wheel, rotating without slipping because of the teeth, inside a larger one that is twice its size. So, the centre of the stub axle moves in a straight line as the geometry dictates. This straight line could be in any direction but, by changing the meshing of the teeth, it can be arranged to be up and down.

The steam cylinder is mounted immediately below it so that the piston rod can be connected, by a bearing, to the axle.

In operation, the arrangement works, as it were, in reverse. As the piston rod is pushed up and down, its upper end constrained to move only in a straight line, it forces the planet wheel to run round inside the fixed large one, carrying with it the disc and the main engine shaft. In theory it was a perfect solution to the problem of converting linear action to rotary motion; sadly, in practice there were problems. Other, quite incidental, factors marred the smooth running of the machine.

James Watt's development of a separate condenser required an air pump as well as the condenser. This pump, driven by the engine, was required to extract the air and water from the condenser and to maintain the vacuum. Murray placed it, together with the condenser itself, in a water filled pit in front of, and underneath, the cylinder. He was then able to connect the pump rod to an extension of the stub axle to which the main piston was connected. Unfortunately, this resulted in all the additional force required to operate the pump being placed on the short bearing of the planet wheel. When the machine had been installed and was working in the tannery, it was soon found that this bearing was inadequate and it quickly became loose and failed. To overcome the defect, Murray or perhaps some ingenious tannery worker, attached a loop of rope to the extended axle. This was brought up to the floor above the machine where it was secured to the end of a strong, pivoted, wooden beam. The other end of the beam had a heavy weight attached so that the whole contraption, acting as a lever, applied an upward force to the axle; cancelling to some extent the extra load imposed upon it by the pump and so relieving the load on the planet wheel bearing.

This machine differed from the standard practice of the day, i.e. from James Watt's designs, in several ways. For example, the valves – or as they were then known – "the nozzles" – offered scope for ingenuity and invention, and steam engine manufacturers vied with each other to design improved versions. Smeaton, in his Portable Engine, some forty years before, had used simple shutters or flaps over the ends of the steam pipes. These were knocked open and shut by heavy weighted levers, tripped by the action of the plug rod.

Murray's hypocycloidal engine used a separate cam shaft driven by a series of gears from the main shaft, like the cam shaft of the modern motor car. Instead of rocker arms, he used a stirrup around each cam. It had an internal projection that was lifted as the high point of the cam passed under it, so operating the valve. He also provided two auxiliary levers by which the valves might be manually operated when starting or stopping the engine.

The bark mill, situated at the back of the machine, consisted of a short, vertical, cast iron, cylinder in which a heavy, fluted, metal cone rotated, driven by massive bevel gears from the engine shaft. Rough oak bark, thrown into the top of the mill was progressively shredded and crushed as it fell down between the rotating cone and the side of the cylinder, emerging underneath the machine as a coarse powder ready for use in the tanning vats. This machine was able to grind up to 4 tons of oak bark in a 12 hour working day.

The machine continued to work in the tannery for several years but by then it was reported that "the joints had become very loose by wearing and the wheelwork went unpleasantly" Presumably it was then scrapped. It was a machine that deserved a better fate. The design was clever and innovative; the whole machine was compact and effective, but it had one small but critical defect. It was the excessive stress on one small bearing, which condemned it.

A small number of hypocycloidal engines were built with minor mechanical changes to improve the planet wheel bearings, but they never became popular.

James Watt's Bell Crank Engine installed in a Scottish Iron Foundry.

Chapter 5

THE SMALL ENGINE

When, at the turn of the Century, the steam engine began to play an increasing part in industry, it became more and more apparent that the size and weight had to be minimised. Instead of the huge stone buildings, housing engines with cylinders up to 8 feet in diameter and with beams weighing many tons, that had characterised the steam engine until then, much smaller self-contained steam power units were wanted. Fenton, Murray and Wood had provided just such a unit in the form of their hypocycloidal engine but they were not alone.

In 1800, James Watt gave up his active participation in the firm of Boulton & Watt and from then on his second in command, William Murdoch, became the driving force in the development of the firm's engines. He clearly saw the need for small power units that could be sited just where they were needed and which were not a fixed part of the structure of the buildings. Murray's hypocycloidal engine met this requirement except in one respect – it had to have a pit in the ground underneath it in which the condenser and the air pump were immersed in water. It was not a totally moveable unit.

The steam supply – the boiler – although in the past it was always built close to the engine it supplied, was now seen as a separate part of the power system. With the use of small steam engines it would be possible to have one boiler supplying several engines, each situated at the place best suited to it.

So the 'Independent Engine' evolved as an engine in which all its parts were supported on an open, iron, cistern or tank. It could be placed just where the user wanted it and it needed no special structural changes to the buildings. All that was required was a constant supply of steam and water. This idea was attractive too from the engine builder's point of view. It was a single entity which he could market as a complete unit and which did not demand much in the way of erection and testing.

William Murdoch, before he was promoted from being Boulton and Watt's representative in the West country to becoming the principal source of the Firm's new engineering developments, had already been thinking along these lines and he was ready with his own design, the 'Bell Crank Engine'. By 1802 Boulton and Watt had developed this into a small free-standing engine. It got its name because the motion of the piston was transferred to the flywheel by means of 'L' shaped levers on either side of the rectangular cistern on which the entire mechanism was mounted.

The name 'Bell crank' stems from the development at about that time, of a system in the great houses of the land, whereby the gentleman, sitting in his drawing room, might summon his servants from the nether regions of the house. By hauling on a bell rope or bell handle he could pull a long wire which stretched all the way to the servants quarters, where it jingled a brass bell. These wires were hidden beneath the floor boards and at every point where they had to go round corners, a little brass lever, with two arms at right angles, was pivoted. It was the 'bell crank'. Hundreds were sometimes used in the big houses so they were a very familiar item to the workmen of those days.

The Bell Crank engine proved a very successful design and Boulton and Watt built and sold a large number. The one illustrated here was built in 1802 and was installed in an iron foundry in Perth; its purpose was to pump a current of air into the blast furnaces. It was slightly different from the general design in that the lower arm of the bell crank was extended horizontally in both directions. One side arm of the crank was pushed and pulled up and down, through a pair of long vertical connecting rods, by the piston in the vertical cylinder above it. Its other end was similarly connected to the piston of a large air pump. The vertical arm of the bell crank, again through two connecting rods, turned the flywheel which provided the momentum required to keep the whole machine turning. The flywheel shaft could also be used to drive another machine.

It is an interesting comment on the business ethics of those days, that Boulton and Watt, when tendering for the business of supplying the engine, provided very clear, detailed, drawings of the site and of all the brickwork of the chimney and engine mountings etc. However details of the engine itself were left vague, and information was confined only to the essentials such as overall dimensions, centre lines of shafts and suchlike. They were not going to reveal any details of their engine that a competitor might steal.

Fortunately for us, a similar engine, built a few years later, is now in the London Science Museum. It has been possible to supplement Boulton and Watts' original drawings with information taken from this engine and to produce a model with fair confidence that it shows a realistic picture of the original engine in its old setting.

The boiler was similar to many others that the firm built; it was a wagon shaped iron vessel supported on brickwork. The furnace underneath the vessel had its flue, before entering the chimney, brought all the way round in the brickwork supporting the boiler drum. Extending from near the bottom of the boiler, and reaching some six feet above, was a vertical standpipe, open at the top. The steam pressure inside the boiler forced the boiling water up the standpipe until the weight of the water column was equal to the steam pressure. Steam pressure rising above four pounds per square inch would have sent scalding water pouring down over the outside of the boiler! and so it was fitted with two safety valves. One was to allow the steam to escape if the pressure inside the boiler became too high and the other was to let air into it if the pressure became too low. The purpose of the first is obvious – accidents did happen and boilers did burst although the pressures used were, by our standards, very low. But boilers were also destroyed by implosion. It was so easy for the engine man, at the end of his day's work, to stop the engine by closing the steam valve, and allow the fire to go out as he went hone to bed. As the boiler cooled and the steam condensed, a partial vacuum would be formed inside the boiler and then the resulting external atmospheric pressure might be sufficient to cause it to collapse – with expensive consequences.

Inside the stand pipe was a heavy stone "float" – it floated because most of its weight was balanced by a chain, passing out of the boiler over a series of pulleys, and connected to a heavy iron plate hanging across the flue. As increasing boiler pressure forced water up into the standpipe, it lifted the float and the plate was lowered into the flue, damping down the fire. It was a primitive, but apparently effective means, of controlling the boiler pressure.

Inside the boiler vessel was another stone float, suspended by a thin rod passing through a gland in the top of the boiler. Its purpose was to open a cock on the water supply so that water from the hot-well could be pumped back into the boiler when the water level was low.

There is a familiar saying that "Nature cannot be scaled". Perhaps it is not exactly true but it does high-light the problems which beset the model engineer when he wants his accurately constructed small replica to behave in the same fashion as its prototype. This model was no exception to that rule.

Since the height of the model boiler is only one twelfth that of its prototype, the boiler working pressure will, in consequence, also be reduced to one twelfth, i.e. to little more than about 0.3 lb/sq.in. – inadequate to work even a model. This problem has been met by sealing off the top of the stand pipe with a spring loaded, corrugated silicone-rubber, diaphragm to which the damper chain is attached. Now the damper is only fully closed only when the pressure reaches about 7 lb/sq.in. Thus a reasonable working pressure can be maintained

This is but one place where Nature refused to be scaled; the chimney was another. The original chimney, was 24ft. high, and so provided a good draught for the real furnace, but that of the model, only 2ft. high, did not. In this case, Nature was given a helping hand by way of a small electric fan, sited out of sight at the base of the tower. The fan was also very effective in creating a realistic plume of smoke!

The development of the steam engine owes much to James Watt's discovery and use of the separate condenser. Yet it is seldom that an effective working condenser is to be found in small model working steam engines. This again can be put down to Nature's intransigence in scaling. Heat exchange requires large working surfaces. The condenser in this steam engine is a large square iron box submerged in water in the cistern on which the machine stands. The exhaust steam from the cylinder passes into it and is condensed, by the cool sides of the box, and so producing a partial vacuum. Additional cooling is provided by a jet of cold water that is sucked in from the tank outside. Hence it is known as a Jet condenser.

In theory, the relationship of volume to surface area in the model should make the small scale condenser more efficient than the full size version. In practice this does not seem to be so, perhaps because the velocity of the steam remains the same whatever the size of the container. Whatever the reason, the model condenser would not work until a series of internal, water filled baffle plates were fitted inside the condenser box. Then a reasonable vacuum developed and the working steam pressure dropped from 7 to 4 lb/sq.in. – a striking confirmation of Watts work.

These modern additions to Watt's engine have been hidden from sight, wherever possible, but they do need control points, pressure gauges and the like. These have all been grouped along one edge of the base of the model where they can be hidden from sight if necessary.

Although not actually a part of the Independent Engine, masonry was an integral part of the engine and its setting. Brick or stone was used according to its availability. In this case it is brickwork. An important feature of brickwork is its bond, the pattern in which the bricks are arranged. All the main walls are 9 inches thick so that the bricks can be laid either along or across the wall, making a number of patterns available to the bricklayer. The two most common are the "English bond" and the "Flemish". Another less common is the "English garden wall bond". This is sometimes known as "Scottish bond". As the foundry was in Scotland, and as Watts did not specify any other, this bond was used for the model, in which there are more than 6500 separate bricks.

Chapter 6

SUGAR and STEAM

The beginning of the nineteenth century saw, in Britain at least, a realisation of the enormous potential of the steam engine; not just in the tin mines of Cornwall, but as a source of energy that would revolutionise the whole world. In the mill and in the factory, in the countryside and even in the colonies, there was need and opportunity for a new source of power, the power of steam.

From its beginning, steam power had required large solid buildings, heavy iron beams slowly moving up and down, and strange and fearsome mechanisms belching out fire and smoke. To become acceptable to the ordinary people of those days, to a population still largely tied to the land and its traditions, steam power had to become more homely and less awe inspiring. It also had to be cheaper than the old familiar forms of power – animal, wind, and water. It was important to reduce size and weight, and of course to cut the cost of new engines.

The need, in Britain's far flung empire, for a convenient source of power was already becoming apparent, particularly in the West Indies where sugar was proving to be a valuable export. Although human slave labour was being horribly exploited to the full in the new colonies, there were situations where machines rather than men had to be used. These had to be driven by mechanical power. Extracting sugar from the stems of the sugar cane was just such a one.

Sugar extraction in the West Indies. London Illustrated News, *1849.*

In the sugar plantations, the freshly cut stems of the sugar cane were crushed between pairs of vertical, fluted, iron rollers, the juice collecting in vats underneath them. This must have been a difficult and dangerous job for the slaves, particularly because the rollers, being vertical, made it difficult to push an even layer of canes between them. The rollers were kept turning by teams of oxen but the use of animal power for this purpose was not to the liking of the plantation owners. The need for power was seasonal, at harvest time, but the oxen had to be fed and watered the whole year. To the plantation owners, steam power must have seemed like a gift from heaven. What was more, the discarded crushed stem of the cane could be burnt in the boiler as fuel costing practically nothing, and the machines themselves would cost nothing whilst they stood idle.

Jukes Coulson of London was one firm that saw the potential of the new market and seized the opportunity. They produced a compact, combined, machine that they exported in considerable numbers to the West Indies from about 1810.

Jukes Coulson, in their design, reverted to the conventional arrangement of an overhead pivoted beam with the steam cylinder at one end and the power take-off at the other. They evidently felt it safe to ignore Pickard's patent and so they used a simple connecting rod and crank together with a heavy flywheel.

The momentum of the flywheel carried the crank over the top and bottom dead centres without any need for Pickard's weighted wheels. The base of the machine was a heavy cast iron cistern, surmounted by a stout iron frame supported on six tall pillars. The beam rocked up and down, supported by the overhead frame. The cistern was filled with cold water that added weight and stability to the machine as well as cooling the condenser that was submerged in it.

The crushing rollers, mounted on their own separate iron frame, making a compact, separate machine, were driven at about one seventh the speed of the engine by a pair of strong gear wheels. A sliding sleeve on the square end of the main shaft allowed the rolls to be disengaged without having to stop the steam engine. The arrangement of three rollers, lying horizontally, with plates to guide the cane into the rolls, was a great improvement on the old vertical, double roller arrangement. It provided that the canes were squeezed twice as they passed between the rolls, and the horizontal rolls and the trays on either side make the presentation of the cane, to the rolls, so very much easier than it had been with the old vertical arrangement.

The boiler was a separate unit, similar in style and action to the one used to drive James Watts' small engine in the Scottish iron works. It too had a damper that controlled the fire in response to the steam pressure in the boiler. In addition, an engine speed regulator was fitted, attached to the framework of the machine over the flywheel. This automatically reduced the steam to the engine as its speed increased. This new device was yet a further step along the path to automatic control. No longer was it necessary for a workman to stand alongside the engine, opening and closing the steam valve as the load on the engine changed. The governor did the job for him.

The governor took the form of a vertical rotating shaft, driven by gearing from the main engine shaft and mounted on the upper frame at the flywheel end of the machine.

At the top of the governor shaft was a short cross-bar, from the ends of which hung two arms with heavy iron balls at their ends. When the engine was stationary, the arms with their balls hung down. As the engine and the shaft started to rotate, centrifugal force caused the balls to swing outwards – the faster the speed, the further the balls spread out, pushing a rod coupled to the steam valve which controlled the steam going into the engine. As the speed increased, so the steam valve closed further, always keeping the engine speed within bounds, It was a very satisfactory form of speed control that became standard practice on most stationary steam engines for a long time thereafter.

This was the beginning of a new age of automatic machine control – machines not only provided power well beyond the limits of human capacity, they took control of it themselves. How proud and how amazed those inventors of the past would be if they see how their primitive methods of control have now been transformed with the advent of modern electronics.

The Sugar Factory.

Chapter 7

PADDLES against PROPELLERS

By the turn of the nineteenth century, steam had become recognised and accepted as a source of power of unimaginable magnitude and versatility, yet one which could be completely under the control of man. Its prospects were endless in the mine and the factory and also, as inventors were quick to recognise, in the field of transport where wind and animal power had hitherto been the only source of energy. However, steam engines and all that went with them were very heavy; dead weights which had to be transported together with the pay load of people or cargo. They also took up a good deal of space. However, the idea of carrying heavy loads, for example of coal, along special tracks of iron rails had already been conceived and found to be practical. Indeed the thought of using coal to carry people on rails was already in people's minds – but that is another story.

Transport by sea, river or canal was a different matter. Ships and barges were themselves large heavy objects; the masts, spars and the sails which drove the ships along were large and heavy components which might be replaced by steam engines without too much change in the proportions of cargo to dead weight. However, the sea involved other considerations as well. On the one hand, wind power came for free but it was also fickle and often dangerous; steam on the other hand, required expensive fuel but its power was always available and predictable. A ship driven by paddles – or in the years to come, by propeller – was much more manoeuvrable at sea than the sailing ship.

On the canal, the other route by which goods were carried around the country, there would be no drag horses which at all times had to be fed and looked after; steam engines cost nothing to keep when they were not in use. But steam power had another less tangible disadvantage, it was feared by the great majority of people. God-fearing, simple folk considered it to be the work of the Devil. There were as well, very many people with vested interests in horse transport, who opposed every aspect of steam powered transport. It was to be a hundred years before steam finally became predominant over sail – and then it too was, in time, to be to be overtaken, first by the internal combustion engine and then by electricity.

Ships driven by paddle are of great antiquity. The Romans used paddle wheels driven by oxen; but with little success, and later the Chinese used men turning handles to drive the wheels. William Symington, in Scotland, is credited with being the first builder of the steam driven paddle ship. His vessel, the CHARLOTTE DUNDAS made its first journey along the Forth and Clyde Canal in 1802. Instead of being hailed as a great new advancement in transport, it was condemned for fear that its wash might damage the banks of the canal. In France and America, attempts were also being made to build paddle steamers; the first successful ship in Europe to carry people was the COMET, built at Glasgow for Henry Bell. In 1812 it carried its first passengers from Glasgow to Greenoch.

Its success prompted the building of a quickly growing number of similar ships or 'Steam Packets' for use on canals and in home waters. RED ROVER was such a one. She was built in 1832 for the London and Herne Bay Steam Packet CO. and together with a sister ship, CITY OF CANTERBURY, made journeys from Herne Bay to London Bridge and back, each day except Sundays. The return journey of some 40 miles took between 4 and 5 hours. It must have been a far more pleasant journey out of London into Kent than by going through the crowded, smelly streets of the East End of London. The ships were met at Herne Bay by stage coaches to take passengers on to Canterbury, Deal or Dover.

Unfortunately for the Steam Packet Co, by 1842 the South Eastern Railway Co. had opened their new line to Ashford and Canterbury; running five trains daily from London into Kent, and giving a faster service than the ships could provide. Also, on the river, another sort of competitor was making its debut; the propeller driven ship. Nevertheless, RED ROVER continued her trips up and down the river, fighting to keep her place against the opposition. There were soon many arguments as to which of the two sorts of ship was the better. To settle the matter, a race was arranged between a paddle steamer and one of the new screw propelled ships. Although RED ROVER was now some 30 years old, she was chosen to race against one of the newcomers, the steam packet MERMAID. It was reported that there was much excitement along the river-side as the two ships, with smoke billowing from their chimneys, challenged each other along a 10 mile course from London Bridge to Long Reach Tavern at Gravesend. The result was inconclusive, with MERMAID crossing the line only 300 yards ahead of her rival after4 a four hour journey. It was a brave showing on the part of the old ship and if her superior manoeuvrability had been taken into account, she might well have been considered the better ship.

    The engines of RED ROVER were typical of her size and type of ship; they were plain and workmanlike. There were none of the Corinthian columns and the elaborate decorations which were to become a feature of later, larger steam ship engines.

    The sea-going steam engines were a variant of the beam engine that was proving so successful on land. But there was a significant difference. On land, in factories and mills, there could be plenty of space between floor and ceiling, that enabled the single large beam to be supported over the cylinders and crank shaft. At sea, head room was very limited indeed; in the cramped space between the decks of a small vessel there was no room for an overhead beam, so, in the sea-going version it was replaced by two beams, low down , one on either side of the engine. These were heavy components and their weight, low down in the ship, contributed to its stability. On the other hand, the large diameter of the paddle wheel made it necessary to have the crankshaft at deck level and consequently, a considerably modified arrangement of Watt's parallel motion links providing straight-line motion for the end of the piston rod had to be fitted. Two engines were fitted along-side each other. The cranks are set at right angles to each other to provide a more even torque through out each revolution. Unlike the beam engine on land, no flywheel was needed; not only did the paddle wheels themselves act as flywheels, the inertia of the ship and the reaction of the water on the wheels ensured steady motion.

With the ship rolling in a heavy swell, the engineer's perch must have been fearsome and precarious. There was little room on the narrow gangway between the two engines, with all their hot pipes and the multiplicity of rods and levers going up and down.

One of the two cylinders and connecting rods.

There is another important difference between sea-going steam engines and land ones. The latter are normally required to rotate in one direction only, but at sea it is essential that the direction of motion can easily be reversed so as to manoeuvre the ship. Early vessels like RED ROVER had a simple, if not very efficient arrangement – the fitting of "slip eccentrics". The eccentric wheels which push and pull the steam valves, instead of being fixed to the crank shaft, are free to rotate between stops approximately half a revolution apart, corresponding to the valve positions for going ahead and for going astern. Once the engine is started running in one direction, the eccentrics slip until they reach the right angular position for that direction and then they can take over by opening the valves at the appropriate points in the cycle. If the engineer has to reverse the direction, he must first cut off the steam to stop the engine. Then, to start it running again in the direction he wants, he must open and close the steam and exhaust valves, by hand, until the eccentrics have slipped round into their correct new positions. From then on, the engine itself can take over the job of operating the valves automatically.

RED ROVER's valves could be operated in this way by levers from the central gangway; but the heavy valves must have required a good deal of brute strength on the part of the engineer, as well as a quick eye to pick the right moments to move them.

Seventy years earlier, James Watt had demonstrated the benefits of a condenser to the steam engine, and this part of the engine had changed little in the course of time. The jet condenser consisted essentially of an iron box, into which the exhaust steam passed, kept cool by a jet of cold water sucked in by the effect of the partial vacuum produced by the condensed steam. This worked well on land where a supply of cold fresh water was available, but at sea, although there was plenty of cold water, it was salt. It was soon found that sea water not only caused corrosion, but choked the condenser with solid salt which had to be cleared out at very frequent intervals. RED ROVER seems to have avoided this problem by flooding the bilges with fresh water when she was at the London Bridge end of her journeys and then using this reserve of fresh water to cool the condenser whilst on the sea leg of the trip.

The paddle wheels fitted to RED ROVER were simple, flat, radial boards attached to an iron framework. As everyone knew, a good oarsman always feathered his oars, twisting them so that the thin edges of the blades entered and left the water with a minimum of splash. RED ROVER's boards hit the water each time with a smack, making plenty of splash and wasting a good deal of energy in the process. Inventors were soon at work producing paddle wheels with pivoted boards that twisted as the wheel rotated, entering and leaving the water cleanly. These wheels contributed significantly to the success of later paddle steamers. If RED ROVER had been fitted with them, her race with MERMAID might well have had a very different conclusion.

There was a problem in presenting the small model as a picture of a real ship. In order that the model engines could be seen in a proper context they had to be fitted into a ship and, of course, if they were to be visible, a good deal of the ship had to be cut away. This led to difficulties in trying to give an illusion of a full sized ship. Hopefully, the pictures will give the impression of RED ROVER as she might have looked many years ago, in the course of construction; propped up by bulks of timber and lying partly built on some riverside shipbuilders hard.

The propeller has now ousted the paddle wheel in all but a few special applications such as dockyard tugs, but many of us will remember with affection the pleasure steamers of the past.

I was born on the Isle of Wight and, in my youth, a special treat was always a trip to Portsmouth on the Paddle Steamer. The attraction was not the scenery – it was to see the engines working. The sight of the huge, polished steel cranks moving inexorably to and fro, the smell of hot oil, and the engineer sitting nonchalantly in charge of all this wonderful machinery, was to me a second heaven. Many men wanted to be an engine driver in their youth. I wanted to be a paddle ship driver!

Chapter 8

THE HORSELESS CARRIAGE

The stories of steam transport by sea and by rail were, as time went by, to become stories of great successes; unfortunately this was not to be the case when steam was applied to transport along the ordinary roads of Britain. The practical and technical problems of using steam to drive small vehicles were difficult but they were not insurmountable; what proved to be the real obstacle was political, it was the power of vested interests. There were too many people, with great influence in politics, who saw steam on the roads as a threat to their power and wealth. They were the winners in the fight to introduce this new mode of transport; within a period of some thirty years, the steam carriage came and then almost disappeared again on the roads of Britain.

It was clear from the start that the conventional steam engine of the time, to be found working away at the pit head or in the factory, was quite unsuitable for a small passenger vehicle. Weight and size had to be drastically reduced. A completely new power unit had to be developed. It was a challenge taken up by many inventors, and their efforts, their ideas, and the solutions they found to the many problems, are a testimony to their ingenuity and foresight. Many of their ideas were since forgotten, only to be resurrected in the motor car of today – albeit, in forms that the originators might have difficulty in recognizing.

The idea of steam driven vehicles on the road was not new; the 'horseless carriage' was envisaged very early in he history of steam. Long before the practical power of steam was demonstrated in the tin mines of Cornwall, Isaac Newton in 1630, inspired by an ancient scientific device, Hero's Aeolipile, made a sketch of a vehicle which, he thought, might be propelled by a jet of steam issuing from a round boiler. In effect, his dream has now become reality in the form of the jet propelled, speed record-breaking, cars of today. What he could never have appreciated was the enormous gap between his scientific knowledge and today's understanding of the natural world which has made his dream come true.

Coming back to more mundane vehicles, the first practical steam carriage was built, in France, by Nicholas Cuignot about 1769. He was an army officer and although he intended his carriage to carry men, his superiors decreed that it should be modified to haul cannon instead. The fate of so many of the early steam vehicles was that minor faults were seized upon, by the detractors of steam, and used to condemn them. This was the fate of Cuignot's vehicle.

By the turn of the century however, many other inventors were suggesting ways of reducing the weight and size of steam engines in order that they might be used to drive carriages. James Watt, in his early days had talked of making his engines "moveable" but the success of his heavy beam engines persuaded him to change his mind and to concentrate upon the machines that were making money for him. However it was William Murdoch, soon after joining the firm of Boulton and Watts, who realized some of the disadvantages of the huge machines and who began to experiment with small engines. He built a toy model vehicle, powered by a tiny boiler and steam engine and he entertained his guests at dinner by making it run along the dining table. The boiler was heated by a candle flame. It is said that, one dark night, he was playing with his toy in the garden when the Vicar called to see him. The poor man, suddenly finding a mysterious light following him up the garden path, took to his heels, convinced that the Devil and the powers of darkness were after him. By this time, James Watt, head of the firm, had lost all interest in steam vehicles and discouraged Murdoch in his experiments so that his work stopped and the idea was dropped.

In Cornwall another enthusiast, Richard Trevithick, was also thinking about steam carriages. He had heard of Murdoch's toy machine and believed that he could do better. His father was 'Captain' of a tin mine near Camborne and he was familiar with the steam engine that pumped water out of his father's mine. At the village school – which he left when he reached ten – he was noted more for his physical strength than for his brains. But he was good with his hands, he was an able mechanic and he had his knowledge of the mine machinery to support his ideas.

With the help of the local blacksmith, John Tyack, he set to work and built a steam powered vehicle. Details now of this first machine are few and shadowy but there is no doubt that it worked. On Christmas Eve, 1801, he put it on the road and with half a dozen of his admirers on board, set off. According to the testimony of one of them later, he trundled along the turnpike at a speed of about eight miles an hour and succeeded in going up Camborne Hill, carrying a number of men, at a good walking pace. It was a great success, and it is remembered in a local song " Going up Camborne Hill, coming down"

    A few days after Christmas, Trevithick, with his cousin Captain Vivian driving, again took the carriage out for another drive, but this time the machine struck a large stone in the road and was damaged. They managed to get the vehicle into a nearby shed and then retired to the local pub to drown their sorrows. They evidently forgot that there were still burning coals in the firebox and when they got back to the shed they found it burnt to the ground and with it their precious carriage.

To Trevithick and his cousin, this was no more than a temporary set-back. They immediately went about the business of preparing and of taking out a patent for a new and, presumably, improved machine. This work was finished by March 1802 when a patent for "Improvements for Steam Engines, etc" was enrolled in their joint names. By now they were persuaded that another steam carriage should be built and, this time, exhibited not in Cornwall but in London. Although the patent is largely concerned with steam engines and boilers in general, it does give comprehensive details of a complete carriage. It is these that form the basis of their "London Carriage".

By February of the following year, the boiler and engine were being built, in Cornwall, whilst in London the rest of the carriage was being put together. The general details of the framework of the machine are clear from the patent drawings but there is a problem with the carriage body – the accommodation for the passengers. The drawings show, in dotted lines only, a structure like the body of a gentleman's coach. Traditionally this was a rectangular box with a curved base and a door on either side. The text of the patent makes it clear however that the drawing does no more than show the designer's intentions. It says, "The body of the carriage may be made of any convenient size or figure, according to its intended uses".

We have no contemporary drawings of Trevithick's carriage, but artist's pictures, made later of the carriage, have always taken the patent drawings literally and have pictured a ordinary coach body perched up in the air between two very large wheels. This must be wrong, since, with this sort of body in this position, the 9ft. high wheels prevent the doors from being opened and, even if they could be opened, make access to them extremely difficult. It is entirely reasonable to assume that this sort of body was not fitted. So what was?

At this stage, I began to look at other contemporary carriage bodies that he might have been used and I found that the very common "Mail Phaeton" body was a perfect fit. Two people could sit comfortably on the driving seat, covered, in bad weather by a leather hood, with a large luggage space behind them. This body even had a cut out section underneath, to clear the front wheels of the coach for which it was intended, which matched exactly part of the steam engine which projected upwards. The Mail Phaeton body might have been made for Trevithick's carriage so this is what I have fitted to the model.

Another interesting anomaly was found in the Patent drawings – showing that even great inventors such as Trevithick could make very human mistakes. The steam valves of the ordinary steam engine of this period – such as those of Red Rover or of the sugar mill – were operated relatively slowly by cams or eccentrics. Trevithick evidently wanted to get as much power as possible from his small engine. He reasoned that if the valves were opened quickly at each appropriate moment instead of gradually, he would get more steam into the engine at each stroke and therefore more power out. So he designed a pair of devices whereby, as the engine shaft rotated, a spring was slowly cocked and then, at exactly the right moment in each cycle, be suddenly released to operate the valve to which it was connected.

At first sight it appeared that, as drawn, his mechanisms would not work. It was only when I realized that Trevithick had got the direction of rotation wrong, that his design made sense. He had evidently forgotten that he had put a pair of spur gears between the engine driving shaft and the wheels, so that when the carriage went forward, the engine had to turn backwards. Putting this right did demand a small change to the design but I am confident that Trevithick would have made the same change when he came to build the carriage.

The essential framework of the machine consisted of two iron girders, lying in a narrow horizontal "A" formation. At the front end, a vertical steering post, attached to a pair of front wheels, had a long tiller that reached back to the driving seat. Between the girders at the rear end was a cylindrical boiler with an internal fire box and flue connected to a tall iron chimney. To conserve heat losses, the steam cylinder was also embedded inside the boiler. The extended piston rod reached forwards, underneath the driver's seat where two connecting rods stretched back to the crankshaft. This had a small gear wheel at both ends, engaging with much bigger gears on the large carriage wheels, which rotated on a fixed axle. The small gears were driven through clutches from the crank shaft, and the driver had two levers with which he could disengage one or other of the wheels when the carriage was turning a corner. The need for one wheel to be able to turn further than the other on curves was recognized, but differential gears for this purpose had not then been invented.

Another lever applied a brake, not to the wheels directly but to the flywheel of the engine and a fourth lever controlled the main steam valve.

Trevithick's carriage weighed more than one ton, and steering this heavy machine by means of a short tiller must have been a Herculean task on the rough, stony roads of Cornwall. If the first steam carriage which ran so blithely up Canborne Hill had, as seems likely, a similar steering arrangement, then this could well have been the cause of the accident. A stone in the road could easily have knocked the steering tiller out of the hands of the driver. It is interesting to see how this very real problem, of steering such heavy vehicles on the rough roads of the time, was tackled by subsequent inventors.

The boiler fire door was at the back of the machine so, presumably, the stoker was expected to walk behind the vehicle, shoveling in coal when it was required. He would also have had the task of seeing that there was enough water in the boiler. For this purpose, two small brass taps were fitted to the back of the boiler, one above the other. If, when they were opened, boiling water issued from the top one, then the boiler was full. If steam only came from the lower one then the boiler needed refilling. This must have been quite a business since, to get more water into the boiler, it had to be allowed to cool until the pressure had dropped to a little below atmospheric pressure so that water could be sucked in through a funnel situated just underneath the carriage body. Not a very practical process!

The heaviest part of a steam power unit is its boiler and Trevithick realized that if it was to be reduced in size and weight for use on the road, then the steam pressure must be as high as was practical. His machine worked at a much higher pressure than other steam engines of the time. It was a brave step forward, in view of the public's fears of steam power, but it was an essential one, and one for which he will always be remembered.

Trevithick's Carriage was an experiment; it could never have been financially viable as it stood and he was unable to raise cash to continue his experiments. Perhaps it was a failure but it was a magnificent one. Beside being a new and outstandingly useful piece of machinery, his carriage has about it a great sense of elegance and beauty which surely makes it a real work of art.

A Model Family.

Chapter 9

MUSKET BARRELS to BOILERS

Trevithick's carriage had been little more than a seven day wonder when completed, as it paraded along a London street, cleared of all horse transport for the occasion. It's inventor had lost interest and moved over to other pursuits and ideas. Perhaps it was a mistake, perhaps if he had continued, the whole history of steam transport on the roads might have been different. As it was, Richard Trevithick's mind was on other projects and ideas. He built no more carriages but went on to build the first steam locomotive. His end was not unlike that of so many of his kind in those days. Twenty years later, living at the Bull Inn in Dartford, he was taken ill whilst working on one of his other inventions. On his death it was found that he did not possess sufficient money even to meet his debts with the innkeeper. He would have been given a pauper's grave if his friends had not together collected sufficient money to give him a decent burial.

If Trevithick had lost interest, others had not, and the following two decades were an incubation period for the development of a multitude of ideas for applying steam to road transport. There were many problems that had to be solved. It is interesting now, with hindsight, to look back and to see that there was one question, which we would now consider as trivial, but which was dominant in so many of the inventor's minds. It centred upon the doubt as to whether, just by making the wheels go round, a vehicle would move along the ground. Many claimed that the wheels would slip and the vehicle would stay still. The argument seems to have been – "Carriages were intended to be moved by some extraneous force, such as, for example, a horse. The wheels were there only to help the carriage to slip easily over the ground. Therefore, the wheels themselves too would slip". It was an age in which "logical" argument carried far more weight than experimentation! So, patents were taken out for carriages in which several pairs of feet, acting like moving legs, were arranged to push them along. It was claimed that this form of propulsion would be far less damaging to the road surface than wheels. In other patents, ordinary road wheels were fitted with spikes or hinged flaps to make them grip the road surface. The idea of a vehicle which laid its own track to run on, was mooted, and yet another machine consisted of a metal drum, some nine feet in diameter and five wide with a wheeled steam carriage inside it. The drum had internal gear teeth matching similar teeth on the carriage wheels so that as the carriage wheels were driven round, the drum and all in it rolled along the ground with an action similar to that of a donkey in a tread mill. This scheme at least had one thing in its favour – as it rolled along it would have smoothed the roughest of roads. However, these ideas were only the fantastic face of invention. Trevithick had already shown that smooth wheels were adequate to propel a carriage on the ordinary road surfaces, and most inventors were generally concerned only to devise ways of countering the worst effects of the dreadful road surfaces.

Julius Griffith was one such. In 1821, he was awarded a patent entitled "Improvements in Steam Carriages" in which he described a machine intended specifically to carry passengers on the common highways. He had a prototype carriage built by Joseph Bramah, a celebrated mechanic of his day and one who is best known today as the inventor of the safe lock. It is doubtful if this carriage was ever driven on the public highway but it seems frequently to have been put through its paces in Bramah's yard and also to have attracted a great deal of attention from other potential carriage builders. It was recorded however, some three years later, as having been modified to carry ordinary goods around the streets of Birmingham.

Apart from the passenger accommodation that consisted of two ordinary coach bodies, all the other details were aimed at providing a machine which was as light and as strong as possible and which at the same time took every advantage of the new form of power.

The body or chassis upon which the carriages, engine and boiler were assembled consisted of two stout, curved, wooden beams, some 15 feet long, joined together at the front end and separated by about five feet at the rear, in the form of a very elongated letter 'A'. A tall, transverse, structure at the front end, attached by a pintle so that it could twist slightly, carried the driver's seat, the steering gear, and a pair of sturdy wheels. At the rear end, a strong bridge supported the entire weight of the engine and boiler. This bridge, consisting of a wooden beam, supported by wooden struts and held together by iron tie rods, was, mechanically, well designed for its purpose. The whole wooden structure is a striking testimony to Griffith's understanding of the stresses that his machine would have to withstand on the rough roads of Britain.

The two coach bodies were mounted between the two vertical structures, each supported underneath by two longitudinal and two transverse, laminated, springs. In this position, the springs would have protected the passengers from the direct shocks of the wheels striking the stones but, being so far below the centre of gravity, would have induced a wild swaying motion.

Trevithick's first carriage probably came to its sad end as a result of the steering being knocked out of the driver's hands by stones in the road. Even the horse drawn stage-coaches were susceptible and could be deflected and even overturned by the stones. An Austrian inventor named Ackermann had, at about this time, suggested a mechanical arrangement of the steering whereby the front wheels of a coach would be less easily deranged by the poor road surfaces. Griffith must have known of this and he designed his steering system along the same lines. The two wheels were individually pivoted, but were moved together by a common track-rod operated by a steering wheel through a reduction gear. So was born the form of steering to be found in millions upon millions of motor cars today – Ackermann steering.

The engine and boiler with its chimney, the pumps, the large condenser and the stoker's seat, in fact the entire power unit as a single compact assembly, was suspended by springs to isolate it from the road shocks. It must have weighed at least a ton and the design of suitable springs was a new and difficult problem. Hitherto, coaches had generally been suspended on what were known as "C" springs – or to older members of our generation as "Pram springs". These were curved leaf springs, at the four corners of the carriage, from which the coach body was suspended by stout leather straps. With the great proliferation of new varieties of horse drawn vehicles at about this time, new forms of springing were being developed, mostly of the sort, loosely called "Telegraph" springs. These steel leaf springs were very much like the ordinary motor car springs of up to a few years ago.

Griffith – great innovator that he was – found quite a different method of springing and of supporting his engine unit. The platform of the power unit was suspended, at each of its four corners, by a pair of chains. The two chains of each pair were shackled together, at the top to iron arms attached to the wooden bridge of the carriage and at the bottom, to the power unit. Midway between top and bottom of the two chains, a horizontal compression coil spring was fitted between them, holding them apart, in effect making each of the chains a kind of bow string. It was a brilliant solution. It was simple, it allowed the unit a great degree of freedom of movement, it was very compact and it required quite small and weak springs to fully support the great weight of the power unit. It had yet another advantage, although it is unlikely that Griffith himself would have fully appreciated it. The characteristics the spring – the relationship between the extent the spring extended and the force applied to it – were far better suited to this application than the more ordinary springing would have been.

Supporting the engine on springs unfortunately brought with it an extra problem. The driving gears and rear wheels were attached directly to the rigid frame of the machine whilst the engine was free to swing around on its chains and so there had to be some form of flexible coupling between them. For this purpose, Griffith fitted what he called his "Artzbergers". He was an honest man and did not try to take credit for other people's ideas which, in this case, originated from an invention, Professor Artzberger of Vienna. They were short axles, attached through universal joint, at one end to the engine and at the other, to the speed reduction gears.

Doctor Church's Phantasmagorian.

Chapter 10

A PHANTASMAGORIAN

By 1830 the idea of a steam powered vehicle, carrying people on the roads had become a reality. The steam train was already beginning to make it possible for considerable numbers of people to move long distances at reasonable cost, but the train needed iron rails – a railroad – and these cost a great deal of money. "Why not" inventors asked, "Use the roads that were already there?" If steam could provide the power to move people on iron rails it could surely move people on roads. It was a very enticing idea; there was clearly money to be made if it succeeded and many engineers and inventors were interested. Heaton, Hancock, Gurney and Maceroni were but some of the well-known engineers of the day who tried their hand at this new way to wealth and fame. All built steam carriages, but one carriage stood out above all others for sheer flamboyance, the wonderful, indeed the awesome machine of Doctor Church. The press named it "Church's Phantasmagorian". This derisory description, and the carriage's size and many embellishments, obscured the fact that it was a most outstanding piece of machinery with engineering concepts far in advance of its time.

Doctor William Church, its creator, was himself an extraordinary man. Born in 1779 in the State of Vermont in America, he spent the first forty years of his life studying medicine and becoming a practising doctor. But his interests lay more with the working of machinery than with the working of the human body. So, in between his doctoring duties, he found time to invent a steam engine, a machine for making nails, a screw propeller, and a breech loading gun. His engineering interests were spread far and wide and they were so important to him that about 1820 he gave up his practice in Boston and came to live in England, then, the centre of engineering of the world. He settled down to live in Birmingham where he became prominent amongst the engineering community. He described himself as an engineer and although he retained his title of "Doctor" he seems to have entirely given up being one. During his stay in this country, he obtained more than twenty patents. They ranged from making buttons to making boilers, from new ways of smelting iron to improvements to the electric telegraph. The whole world of engineering was his.

One of his brain children was to be of outstanding importance in the changes to the world that were going on around him. He invented the first type setting machine.

Caxton's invention of the printing press, with all its power to influence public opinion and to disseminate information, has been an inestimable force for change.

In Church's day, little had changed with the machine itself since Caxton's time. Printers were still preparing their presses by selecting, one by one, little wooden or lead letters –'type' – from a group of boxes and then arranging them one by one to compose the messages they would send out into the world. At the beginning of the nineteenth century, newspapers were printing hundreds of thousands of words each day. Each letter had to be laboriously selected from its little box and clamped up into the forme before the printing could be done. The printers became extremely quick at the process. However, when the printing was over, each letter had then to be taken out and examined or identified before it could be put back into its proper box. This was an even greater task than setting the type and, from the point of view of the newspaper owners, an unwanted extra expense. Church suggested a radical change. Why not have a machine which, at the touch of a key, selected and then allowed each individual letter to fall from its little box into place in the forme. When the printing was done, the printer could simply melt all of the type down into a lump of metal. Then another machine would reuse the metal, cast a new lot of type in groups of each letter and then put the groups back, each in its appropriate little box?

He designed, in great detail, each of the two special machines and, for good measure, a new sort of printing press in which to use his new type. The national press welcomed the idea with open arms; it was just what they wanted. But, as has been so often the case, the story of this most important invention had a sad ending. Someone else stole his ideas and got all the credit and the gain. Church got nothing. It is said of him that he was of gentle and trusting nature and, contrary to the very aggressive nature of business in his day, he never went to law to protect himself.

This misfortune did not stop him. His mind was so full of new ideas that he was forever dropping what he was working on and jumping to the next invention. He too felt the challenge to build a steam carriage and it was not long before his version was under construction. Like Griffith's carriage before him, this new carriage was also built in Bramah's Yard in Birmingham.

Engineers in his day had to be men of many parts; it is likely that the explicit and beautifully clear drawings that accompany all of Church's Patent applications were the work of his own hands. The text itself may well be that of an expert lawyer writing on his behalf. Engineering drawing was much less formalised then than it is now. In 1830 it more often had the hall mark of an artist than of a mechanic. Church demonstrates this so delightfully in his patents by the little drawings of the men in his machines.

Church's carriage, or "diligence", which eventually emerged from Bramah's Yard, was an enormous machine, some 30 feet long and 7 feet wide. Weighing several tons, this highly decorated Colossis rolled along on three wheels. They were not ordinary wheels but special ones that Church thought would spare his carriage from some of the worst effects of the road surface. The two driving wheels, seven feet in diameter, had their rims made up of thin wooden laminations with a thin protective iron tread that flattened out in contact with the ground. Instead of the conventional wooden spokes, they had 32 thin flat steel springs – the entire wheel was, to some extent, flexible. To supplement the wheel's shock absorbing qualities, the axles themselves were supported by air pressure acting on the pistons in two pneumatic cylinders. As a further protection against obstacles in the road, triangular deflector plates were hung in front of the wheels to knock the biggest of the stones out of the way.

The driver sat high up at the front of the vehicle and, on a seat at the rear, was perched the guard. Hidden inside, between the boilers and the engines, was the engineer. His must have been a very restricted, hot and uncomfortable post but he was not entirely isolated from the outside, Church had kindly provided him with a speaking tube so that he could talk to the driver! The passengers sat in two small compartments, one in front and the other behind the "engine room"; those in the rear being favoured with a view of the engines in operation.

The single wheel, at the front of the carriage, was held in a circular framework that could be turned to right or left to steer the carriage by means of a pinion and large gear wheel. The interesting thing here is that the pinion – the small gear wheel turned by the steering handle – had only two teeth. Insignificant as this might seem, only when the model was completed was its importance discovered. As the steering handles and the small gear wheel were turned, they passed through two diametrically opposite positions in each revolution where the framework carrying the front wheel was completely locked against the kind of derangement that had upset Richard Trevithick's carriage on Christmas Eve. It was just one more example of Church's foresight.

Strength was the keynote in the design of the body. It was built up of a huge framework of wooden spars, designed as Church explained, "that each timber, rib, rail, rod, tube or bar may receive and sustain its due proportion of weight or strain". Timbers were not to be mortised or dove-tailed as this might reduce their strength; instead he designed special metal strips to join them together. Such was his love of decoration, that even these, hidden out of sight behind the outer skin of the vehicle, had to be fancifully shaped! The framework alone is a revealing indication of Dr Church's innate sense of good design.

Each of the two driving wheels had its own engine and boiler although the driving shafts were in fact coupled together. It is not surprising, in the light of Church's ingenuity, that the boiler, and the engine, was different from any that had gone before.

The engine cylinders were hung from pivots on stout supporting timbers and as the crankshaft revolved, swung to and fro. This eliminated the need for connecting rods and made the engine very compact. The drive from each engine to the road wheel was by two pairs of chain wheels; either could be selected by the engineer to give the vehicle two gear ratios. There were neither brakes nor differential gear, but either wheel could be disconnected from the engine for making sharp turns.

The two vertical boilers had a complicated system of water siphons and smoke tubes and a central coal hopper that had to be filled – most inconveniently – from just under the roof of the engine cabin. The boilers were yet one more testimony to Church's ingenuity; the ultimate example of this must surely be his forced draught fans.

Instead of a common or garden chimney pot, Church, with all of his sense of elaborate display, provided a stupendous polished copper dome from which smoke must have billowed as from an enormous censer. It was not an ordinary chimney, it concealed two rotating fans, coupled together, each inside a circular chamber. The bottom fan was driven by jets of exhaust steam from the engine. It was in effect a turbine. The result of the jets and the rotation was to suck the smoke from the boiler and expel it out from the chimney. The other fan ventilated the front passenger coach by sucking air from it and then forcing it through pipes leading down to beneath the fire grate, thus providing the fire with forced draught as well. Without question, this must be the first attempt at what we today think of as the ultimate in modern car engine design; it was a turbo charged engine in 1830.

It was interesting to find, when the model was tested, that the force of the exhaust steam alone was insufficient to drive the fan adequately. Church must have found the same problem because his design shows a supplementary driving belt from the engine to get additional power to drive the fans.

Not much is known about the fate of this beautiful invention of Doctor Church. The newspapers reported it as making some runs on the Coventry Road, and its builder had high hopes of starting a service to London with it, but it is unlikely that it ever got so far afield as that. However he did issue a prospectus for the "London and Birmingham Steam Carriage Company". The last news of Dr Church's glorious Phantasmagorian was that it was lying abandoned in a country lane outside Birmingham. The size, weight and cumbersomeness of this strange machine made it almost a non-starter in the competition, in the early eighteen hundreds, to develop mechanical road transport. Its patent disadvantages were a convenient point of attack for the detractors of the new means of locomotion, to seize on. Despite all of its faults, we can today recognise the genius of the gentle American doctor.

His story ended as did so many others to whom, today, we owe a debt of gratitude and an acknowledgement of their genius. At the age of 80, ill and with no money, his friends in Birmingham collected sufficient money for his fare back to his son's house in America, where he died on the 7th October, 1863.

Chapter 11

A FORETASTE of the FUTURE

By about 1830, enthusiasm for the idea of steam on the road was reaching its peak, both amongst inventors and visionaries of all sorts. There were also the hard headed business men who saw in it a good prospect of making a lot of money if they could find the right man to back. James and Anderson were two such people.

William Henry James, of Winson Green, described as a 'Gentleman of superior mechanical talents; a Civil Engineer', was the one who supplied the inventive and engineering ideas to the pair. Sir James Anderson, put up the money.

James concept of a steam driven conveyance was different from that of most others. He believed that, just as horses pulled the carriage in which the passengers sat, so also the steam engine should be a separate unit, pulling the passengers behind in their own carriage; just as the new steam trains were doing.

As early as 1824, James had obtained a patent for a steam vehicle that had many entirely novel and clever new features. For example instead of a single steam engine it had four, each with two cylinders, attached individually to each of the four wheels. The two engines on one side of the machine were connected to the boiler by one pipe and stop cock, and the other two engines through another, separate, pipe. The engines had very small cylinders and were expected to work at the high pressure of 200psi. The front axle of the vehicle could be turned by a steering wheel, but James added another device. The two steam cocks of the engines were connected to vehicle's steering so that if the vehicle was turned to the right, steam was reduced to the engines on the right and increased to those on the left, and vice versa when steered to the left. In one brilliant idea, he had anticipated both the differential gear and the power steering of the modern motor car. It was reported that, when trials of this arrangement were carried out later, the carriage was able to make to make turns of only 10 feet radius, as well as carrying out other tightly convoluted movements.

Like so many other inventors, William James was full of new ideas but he had very little money to convert his ideas in to reality. James Anderson, Bart. of Bultevant Castle, in Ireland, had money and also a firm belief in the future of steam transport. He recognised James' genius and come to his aid, advancing sufficient money to enable a more realistic version of James' first steam carriage to be built.

This machine made a number of trial runs in Epping Forest and, in spite of frequent boiler problems because of the very high steam pressure, showed great promise. The pair of entrepreneurs planned a steam coach service between Birmingham and London, and James then designed what was undoubtedly the most up to date steam engine for service with it. In accord with his basic principles, his steam engine, which he called a "Steam Drag", drew behind it an omnibus body of the sort normally drawn by horses.

Work on the new version was put in hand and went well but it was to prove an expensive venture; Anderson said later that his "apprenticeship with steam engines, cost him £30,000". Money, at least temporarily, ran out and the brave new machine was never quite completed.

The model has been built, as near as the limitations of size would permit, to the very clear and detailed drawings given in the Patent description; its building has revealed many instances of the designer's forward thinking and his appreciation of the very many problems of mechanical road transport.

Even at first sight, the steam drag can be seen to have some unusual features. Other contemporary steam carriages had steering handles or steering wheels which, like today's motor car, turned in a horizontal plane; he provided a steering column in front of the driver with steering handles on either side, moving in a vertical plane. The handles, through gearing, turned a lead-screw that in turn slowly moved the front axle so as to steer the machine. This provided a steering system that was rigid enough not to be easily deflected by stones in the road, which reduced the physical effort of steering, but which required a considerable number of revolutions of the steering handles to turn the vehicle. James evidently realised that the forward and backward action of the human arms, in movements of this sort, was much better than making the twisting action required with a steering wheel.

An attractive and unusual feature of the drag was the row of three magnificent copper "headlamps". The ordinary horse carriages of the time were often furnished with lamps, both to illuminate the road and to provide light for the occupants, They were lit by candles. James was really up to date, he had his lamps lit by coal gas.

By the turn of the century, the use of coal gas was well established in some of the large country houses and it was replacing the candles in their grand rooms. The gas was produced on the estate. Mill and factory owners were finding that they could extend the working day with this new form of lighting. In 1830 gas lighting was becoming one of the 'hi-tech' features of the time. James realised, not only the value of its improved lighting, but of its power to impress his customers. So coal gas was compressed and stored in a container under the lamps. The machine with its brightly shining lamps with their bat wing burners, would have been a magnificent spectacle at night in a dark country lane. The lamps were not the only means of drawing attention to the machine; a large brass trumpet, mounted at the rear, where it could be operated by the stoker, could be sounded, not by the stoker's lungs but by the full power of steam.

The driver not only used his hands for steering, he also was able to make use of his feet to control the machine. By pressing with his heels on a bar passing across underneath his seat he could apply a band brake to the engine's intermediate shaft to slow or stop it, and by engaging his toes in one of three foot pedals, he could change gears whilst still in motion. The pedals were shaped like stirrups so that the driver could also pull them back with his toes. With Griffith's, carriage for example, built ten years before, it had been necessary for the driver to stop and get down to the ground when he wanted to change gears or to put the brake on the wheels.

James provided a three- speed gear change. The engine crankshaft was connected to an intermediate shaft, situated underneath it, by three pairs of chain wheels having different teeth ratios. Each pair of wheels had its independent clutch, and could be selected by pushing down one of the three stirrups. With this arrangement, it would be possible to have two or even three separate sets of gears engaged at the same time, stopping the engine. So he arranged that one of each set of chain wheels should be driven by a ratchet wheel and pawl. If two sets of chain wheels were engaged by accident, then the faster of the two sets simply over-ran the slower one and the engine did not stop. The driver would probably have been warned of his mistake by the noise of the pawls clicking over the teeth.

The intermediate engine shaft drove the two back wheels independently, again by a clutch and chain drive, but here the clutches were connected to the front wheel axle. When the machine was going straight ahead, both clutches were engaged and both wheels were driving it along. When the axle was displaced to go round a bend, the inner wheel was automatically de-clutched since it had to travel a shorter distance than the outer one.The engine, fixed on top of the boiler was of fairly ordinary design, with two inclined cylinders. It could be started or stopped by either the driver or, if he was too busy steering, by the stoker. Let us hope that in an emergency they both thought and reacted alike.

Like the engine, the boiler and boiler system, bore all the marks of James' individuality. It consisted of three cast iron sections, bolted one above the other, There were side covers, and with space between the sections for the fire and hot gases. The iron sections were cored with numerous passages for the steam and water and they were all connected to two vertical steam reservoirs or collecting towers.

The bottom section had a space at one end with fire bars where the fire was contained, the hot gases passing between it and the middle section and then back in the space between middle and top sections before coming out of the chimney. This arrangement provided a very efficient transfer of heat from the fire into the bottom two sections and some degree of superheat into the top.

A hand pump, operated by the stoker, returned feed water to the boiler when it was needed and a double acting leather bellows, driven from the intermediate engine shaft, blew air into the ashes pit, giving forced draught when the engine was running. A length of canvas water hose was attached so that the hand pump could also be used to pick up water from roadside streams when the opportunity arose.

Coal was stored in a bunker underneath the boiler. Instead of having to use a shovel to put coal into the fire, the stoker had only to turn a handle and an iron plate behind the coal, pushed it up a ramp into the fire box. Stoking in the normal way might have been a trifle difficult for the poor stoker, perched precariously on his tiny seat at the rear of the engine.

Exhaust steam from the engine passed into the two condensers – copper boxes on either side of the boiler containing feed water for the boilers. The steam passed into a nest of pipes immersed in the water and was partly condensed; the remainder of the steam going into the chimney to induce further draught for the fire.

The condensate ran into a separate chamber underneath the condenser, from whence it would be returned, when the stoker deemed it to be necessary, into the boiler.

James Steam Drag.

The process of feeding the condensate into the boiler against the steam pressure was ingenious but cumbersome. Beneath the boiler was what James called "the intermediate chamber" – a pressure vessel built up of some 30 pieces of copper pipe attached to headers. James, like most of the steam carriage builders of his time, was well aware of the danger of exploding boiler drums and believed that this was a much safer arrangement than the conventional iron vessel. The tubes in this case had an additional function; they were to facilitate cooling. A pipe, with a stop cock, connected the tubes to the top of the boiler so that, when the stop cock was open, the tubes were at boiler pressure. Another pipe and stop cock connected the tubes to a hand pump, by means of which the stoker could pump the contents back into the boiler when he thought it necessary. Because the pressures had been equalised, this was no hard job. When the contents of the intermediate vessel had been pumped back into the boiler as feed water, the stoker pulled a single lever that did several things at once. It closed the stop-cock between the intermediate vessel and the boiler and also that between the pump and boiler. It opened a stop-cock, in a pipe going between the chamber under the condenser and the intermediate vessel, causing the pressure in the latter to drop to atmospheric pressure. Finally, it also moved a shutter that diverted the blast of air coming from the bellows, on to the surface of the tubes. This lowered their temperature still further so that the condensate was actually sucked back into the intermediate vessel. When the stoker was satisfied that the process was completed, he simply pushed the lever back into its earlier position, reversing the cocks and air shutter and returning to the status quo, except that the boiler now had the extra feed water in it.

Of course it is easy now, with hindsight, to see that a simple feed pump would have done the job much better, but it is yet one more example of James ingenuity and originality.

It is a great pity that James Drag never went on the road, or if it did, that we have no reports on its performance. It was small and compact, well engineered and well thought out, and it could have been much more manageable in the narrow streets and country lanes of nineteenth century England than some of its competitors.

But it was not to be. The opposition to steam on the roads of Britain was all-powerful; the land owners did not want the cost of improving the roads on their land and neither did the villagers whose duty it was to maintain the public roads through their villages. It is reported that, in England at that time, there were about 300,000 horses kept for the purpose of transport. With all the auxiliary industries, stables, harness manufacturers, fodder providers and the like, this represented a huge number of people whose interests were at risk from this new machine and they, to a man, put every obstacle in way of its development.

By the beginning of 1840, most of the brave new 'Steam Transport Companies' had disappeared; only a few dedicated and persistent people were still convinced that steam might yet have major place on the roads. That hope finally faded away with the development of the internal combustion engine. But, despite its failure, the initial development of the steam engine for this new and very difficult role was a very great achievement. It sowed the seed for many of the features of today's motor car.

Chapter 12

THE GAS ENGINE

During the three or four decades that followed Trevethick's demonstration on Camborne Hill of a carriage driven by steam, many people concerned themselves with finding ways of improving the steam engine to make it more suitable for this new application. The future of the steam carriage looked good. But others were aware of the inherent difficulties of steam and searched for other and better sources of mechanical power.

Two thousand years earlier, Heron of Alexandria, beside making his strange Aerolipile – the little steam jet propelled toy – had also contrived machines in which heated air was used to open and close the temple doors and to pour libations of wine on to the altars of the gods. During the seventeenth century, when Heron's writings became known in Europe, his ideas and methods were again put to use and a number of machines were made for raising and moving water by the heating and cooling of air. Then Boyle, Guy-Lussac, Charles, and others discovered laws which explained the behaviour of gases; and so the science of thermo-dynamics began to take shape. It began to be understood that the steam engine was only one form of a heat engine and that hot air engines were another form that might well have something better to offer as a source of power for road transport.

One of the first opportunists who hoped to make his name and fortune by developing heated air machines was a one time cooper, Samuel Brown, with works at Eagle Lodge, Old Brompton, Middlesex. In 1823, he filed a first Patent Application in which he described two separate forms of his "Gas Vacuum Engines". Copies of his patent drawings are shown.

Like Joseph Wrigley before him, he saw the water wheel as one way of obtaining rotary motion from the pressure changes that occurred when air was heated or cooled. Wrigley heated and cooled steam to create a partial vacuum to suck water up into a vessel, from which it was then allowed to run down over a waterwheel that could then drive other machines. Brown used hot air to produce a partial vacuum to suck up the water. He was not a theorist and it seems that he was not too sure of the way in which the vacuum was formed. His abbreviated description of the process in the Patent reads as follows "Inflamable gas is introduced into an open cylinder. A flame then ignites the gas and then the cylinder is closed airtight. Gas continues to flow for a short time and then it is cut off. During that time, by its combustion it acts upon the air in the cylinder. At the same time a part of the rarefied air escapes through a valve and so a vacuum is effected". It is not a very satisfying explanation!

One commentator at the time was apparently quite clear what was meant. Seizing on the word "combustion" he explained "The engine – – – is actuated by the inflammation of hydrogen gas in a vessel containing a portion of atmospheric air, sufficient for the combustion of the hydrogen. The oxygen of the air, thus combining with the hydrogen, together form water which of course, occupying less space than these in their original form, leave in the vessel a partial vacuum". This may well have been Brown's original explanation but it is evident from the way in which his later machines were developed, that he eventually realised that it was predominantly heat and not chemical change that produced the pressure changes by means of which his engines were driven.

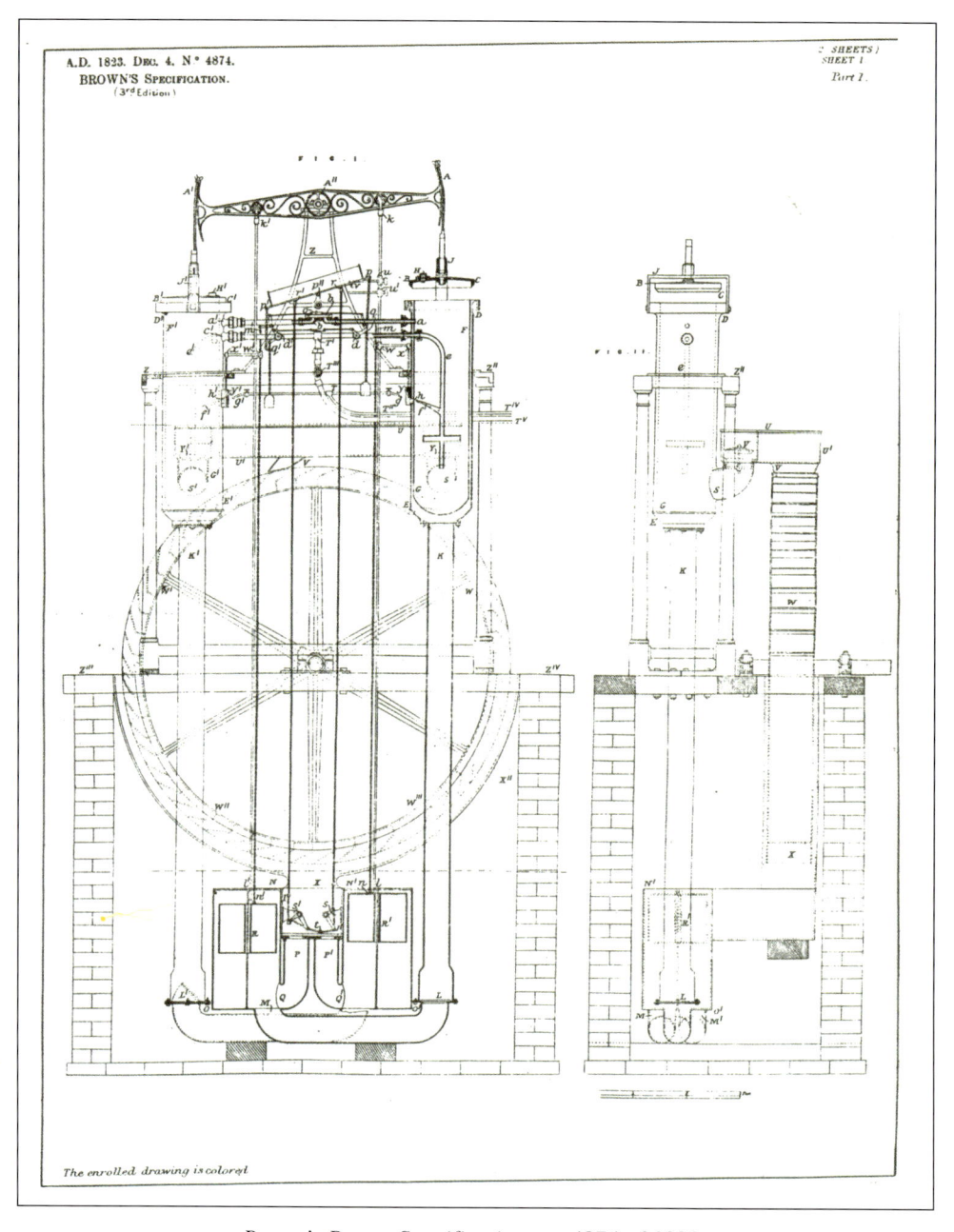

Brown's Patent Specification no. 4874 of 1823.

He is reported as having built and demonstrated a model of the water wheel version of his gas vacuum engines which gave rise to considerable interest in the scientific community. Like much of the popular newspaper reporting of his day, in records of scientific matters it is often difficult to separate objective observations away from the extravagant claims of the innovator. In Brown's case, as it stood, the model of his first machine would not have worked. This was not for any fundamental reason but for the simple practical one that, as drawn, the machine would not have been able to hold sufficient water to work all the various pistons and floats as well as having sufficient left over to fill and turn the wheel. Doubtless, in his demonstration model these and other snags had been dealt with. Nevertheless, some months later, another interested amateur scientist wrote that he had built Brown's machine but that he had got nothing but flames and explosions from it.

The water wheel engine has two tall cylindrical vessels standing above and in front of a large water wheel. Each vessel has a lid, hanging from a pivoted beam above and a foot pipe going down to an open tank at floor level. The foot pipes are transposed so that the right hand vessel goes to the base of the left hand tank and visa versa. Each tank contains a large float attached by long metal rods to the beam above; and an inlet pipe, with a flap valve, connecting it to a water reservoir. The foot pipes each have a non-return valve so that water can pass up the pipes into the vessels above but cannot return. The relative position of the floats causes the beam to tilt; closing one or other of the lids and also opening a series of valves which control the various gas jets. The way that this part of the operation is effected is new and interesting. A long horizontal tube, pivoted at the middle and able to tilt few degrees up or down, contains a quantity of mercury. It has an arm at one end which lies between two stop pins on one of the rods attached to the beam and, as the rod moves upwards with the beam, it lifts that end of the mercury tube until it reaches a horizontal position. At this moment, the mercury commences to run down the tube and it over-balances so as to tilt to its full limit in the opposite direction, giving a "snap" action to the gas taps that are connected to it.

Brown's water wheel engine is supposed to operate as follows. The tanks and lower parts of the foot pipes are filled with water so that the two floats hold the beam level, and then gas – in the case of Brown's first patent, this is assumed to be hydrogen – is turned on to jets inside the vessels. Then some of the water in one of the tanks, for example, the left hand one, is allowed to drain away, causing its float to sink and to pull down the beam, so dropping the lid on the vessel above it. The foot pipe of this vessel, it will be remembered, is connected to the opposite tank. As the beam drops, it momentarily opens a shutter in the side of the vessel, close to which a flame is burning. This ignites the gas inside the vessel. At the same time, the gas coming into the vessel is then cut off by another valve, operated by the mercury tube. As the hot air and the products of combustion in the vessel cool, water is sucked up from the right hand tank, causing its float to fall and to pull the beam down. This then repeats the cycle of ignition of gas and subsequent vacuum on the right hand side. Whilst this is happening, water in the tank on the left hand side is being replenished from the reservoir through another flap valve, also operated by the beam. The cycle of operations is continuous, first on one side and then on the other. Each cycle sucks more water up the foot pipes until it reaches an exit valve, opening out into the leet of the water wheel, setting the whole machine in motion. Water in the system is continuously replenished – hopefully – from the reservoir into which the water from the wheel falls.

In practice, particularly with both my small scale models, the mode of operation is far from the simple process that Brown described. The major problem is in igniting the gas and having it burn peaceably – it usually does not catch fire when it should, or else it does so with a violent explosion. The inventor suggested that air should be mixed with the hydrogen as an economy measure but even his enthusiasm did not go so far as to recommend that the explosive mixture should be stored under pressure in a closed vessel. It seems unlikely that engines in this form were ever successfully used to turn rotary machinery but there are records of water pumping engines using a somewhat similar mode of operation.

The other version of Brown's gas vacuum engine, shown in his Patent no. 4574, looks a little more like the small steam engines that James Watt and others were currently building. A heavy rectangular iron tank with tall pillars at the corners and two vertical cylinders supports a sturdy overhead beam from which hang chains attached to pistons in the cylinders. The beam is pulled down, first on one side and then the other by the action of a partial vacuum, produced alternately beneath the two pistons. Two connecting rods and a flywheel and crankshaft, lying across the tank, convert the movements of the beam into rotary motion. Ignition ports in the sides of the cylinders are opened and closed by rods from the beam and a mercury tube mechanism, similar to that in the water wheel engine, operates the various gas valves.

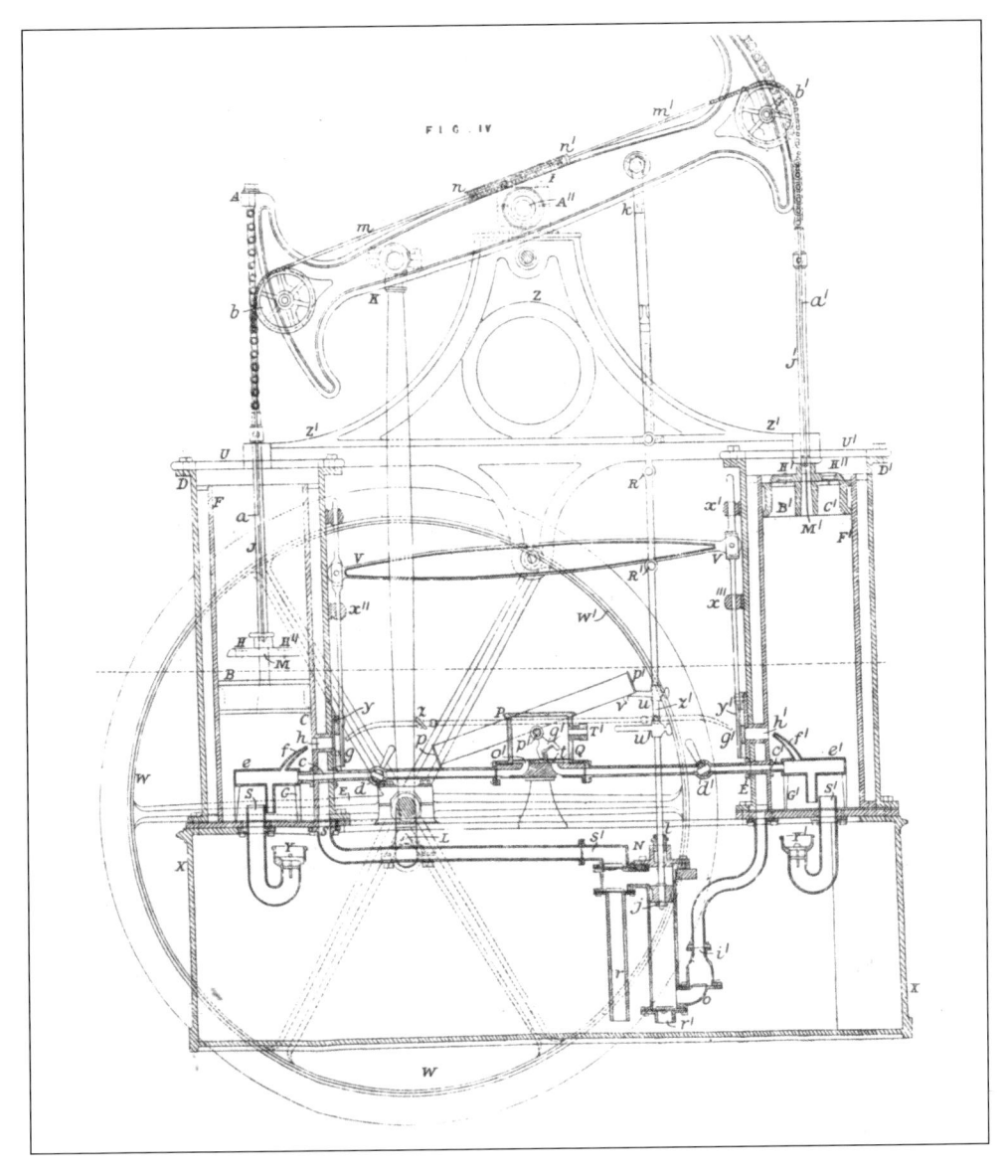

The working principles are the same as in the other machine. The cylinders themselves are water-cooled. Gas is admitted and ignited as the pistons move upwards. At the top of the stroke, flap valves in the piston heads and the ignition aperture in the cylinder wall, close, and the cooling of the gases, helped by the water-cooled walls of the cylinder results in a reduced pressure that pulls the piston down again. All together, this is a more workable machine than the water wheel. However, like the other machine, the model, still has difficult ignition problems.

In 1826 Brown took out another Patent, No. 5350, in which he described a more sophisticated version of this gas vacuum engine. A small ship was purchased; one of his new engines was installed driving a screw propeller in the bow, and, amid much publicity, a trial run along the Thames was made, attended by no less than the Lords of the Admiralty. After some initial problems the ship made up to seven knots but only as long as the gas lasted, which apparently was not very long. Brown hailed the run as a great success but it seems that My Lords were not so impressed when they learned of the cost of the gas, and the firm that Brown had floated to finance this great new invention had to be dissolved.

The gas vacuum engine was a brave new attempt to find new sources of power; it was over publicised at its onset and, when it failed to meet the extravagant claims made for it, condemned too harshly. Brown did, in fact, have some success with his engines. One was put into service raising water from a canal at Croyden and he had another working in his own works at Brompton. He built a plant to make his own coal gas to run the machine and he claimed that, after he had sold the coke from the gas plant, his running costs were some £150 per annum less than would have been the case for a comparable steam engine. What ever the success or otherwise of Brown's Gas Vacuum engines, they stand out as a very important part in the development in a new sort of engine, the hot air engine; an engine which even today, plays its part in modern space technology.

Samuel Brown's Gas Powered Water Wheel.

Chapter 13

THE FIRST ELECTRIC TRAIN

By the beginning of the nineteenth century, the enormous potential of steam had been exploited in every direction, in the mines and factories, and in transport both by land and sea. Indeed, visionaries were even contemplating steam-powered balloons to carry goods by air. Steam was the power to revolutionise the world. But another force was emerging from the workshops of the philosopher and scientist; it was electricity. Of course it was not new; the power of the thunderbolt and of the lightning flash had been known and feared since time began; however, that was the power of the Gods, not of man.

Nevertheless, people like Otto von Guericke were already beginning to make machines, in which friction applied to substances such as sulphur, produced electric sparks looking like miniature versions of lightning. Then, in 1751, Benjamin Franklin, Deputy Postmaster of Philadelphia, carried out his famous experiments of flying a kite in a thunderstorm. He demonstrated that the electricity that he collected from the lightning storms via his kite string was indeed alike, at least in nature if not in magnitude, with man-made electricity. Spectacular as these experiments may have been, they showed no prospect of competing against the power of steam. It was the twitching of a frog's leg which heralded the coming of a new and totally different way of harnessing the world's sources of energy.

In 1791, an Italian physiologist, Luigi Galvani was investigating the anatomy of a frog's leg when he noticed that part of the dead frog twitched when he touched it with his steel scalpel. He suggested that this movement of the dead animal might be due to the presence of "animal electricity". But a countryman of his at the University of Parva, Alessandro Volta, was able to show that the electricity resulted, not from animal activity but from chemical activity. He went on to develop the first 'voltaic' cells and to demonstrate that electricity – the power of the Gods – might be obtained at will from simple substances here on earth. The 'voltaic pile' was described by Volta in 1800.

All this was far removed from the mechanical nature of the steam engine, with its wheels that went round and its rods which pushed to and fro, until Hans Anderson Oersted discovered the magnetic effects of electricity. He demonstrated that electricity could produce mechanical forces, although, in his experiments the forces were very small indeed. This was in 1820. Who at that time could have even dreamed that these tiny effects, detectable only in the laboratory, would in the short space of twenty years, be so far developed that they would drive a railway train weighing 5 tons? The man who brought about this astounding event was not a Michael Faraday, or any other of the celebrities of the scientific world, but an obscure Scottish yeast manufacturer and part-time dentist.

Robert Davidson, born in Aberdeen in 1804, the son of a grocer, had a far-reaching interest in the science of his time. Apart from his dentistry, for which he made his own equipment, he built a 40 ft telescope in his garden and he experimented with the production of new chemical dyes. As a young man, he had attended the University of Aberdeen, but had not succeeded in graduating. It seems he was more interested in making scientific machines than in studying them; but by building apparatus for his teachers – for example he built a steam engine for one of the Professors – he made influential friends in the University. Electricity was then becoming a subject of great interest to the scientific world and Davidson was stirred by the more practical aspects of this new wonder. He must have learned, through his friends at the University, of the efforts of people such as Faraday in London, of Jacobi in Russia, and of others who were trying to bring the potential power of electricity into everyday use. As early as 1837 he had constructed simple batteries and an electric motor sufficiently powerful to drive a lathe or even a printing press. The best efforts of other scientists, in this country at least, had resulted in machines which, more or less, just demonstrated that they could spin round. One was powerful enough to turn a roasting spit, but mostly they were little more than scientific devices. Davidson, on the other hand had, by 1840, working away quietly and more or less unnoticed in Aberdeen, built and demonstrated an electric locomotive weighing around 5 tons. The new railway line between Edinburgh and Glasgow had just been opened and he was allowed to try it out there, where it succeeded in running for a mile and a quarter at a speed of up to 4 mph. Looked at in the light of today's technology, this was an astounding achievement and it was one that has never received the acclaim it so well deserved.

In the early 1800's, steam railways were proliferating throughout the land and in February 1842, the Edinburgh and Glasgow Railway was opened. It offered four classes of travel; first, second, third, and fourth. In the first class carriages, folk travelled in comfort, sitting on comfortable seats where they were fully protected against the weather. In the second class they had to stand, unless they had brought their stools with them, but at least they had a roof over their heads. But the third and fourth class passengers had to stand in open trucks, exposed to the rain and to the black smoke and cinders from the engine. Passengers in the new steam trains could not have found travel, with steam, very comfortable. Robert Davidson was convinced that for the new railways, his electric locomotive was far better than the steam ones. It has taken more than a hundred years to prove him right.

Davidson was a man of high principles and he refused to patent any of his new ideas and machines. He strongly believed that the whole of humanity should freely have the benefits of science; that it was the duty of those people blessed with the gift of knowledge and ingenuity to give their services to improve the lot of mankind; not just to make as much money as they could from their ideas. It is sad to think that, had he been a little more mercenary and had he patented his ideas, they would have been recorded by the Patent Office and he would have been far better known today. He would have been given much more of the credit his work deserved. As it is, records of his work are scarce, mostly coming from newspaper reports that, when dealing with scientific matters in those days, tended to be unreliable. Most of the information available today comes from a friend of his at the University, Dr David Mackie, Lecturer on Mechanical Philosophy. Not surprisingly, considering the extent of scientific knowledge at the time, some of Dr Mackie's information is confusing and misleading, and in trying to build a coherent picture of Davidson's locomotive it has been necessary to look at some of his details in the light of today's technology. This means that it was sometimes necessary to amend and improvise on his descriptions. There are no Patent drawings to work from, but there are two other drawings that are relevant. One, made by Dr Mackie, is of a four-wheeled cart containing two of Davidson's motors attached directly to the wheels.

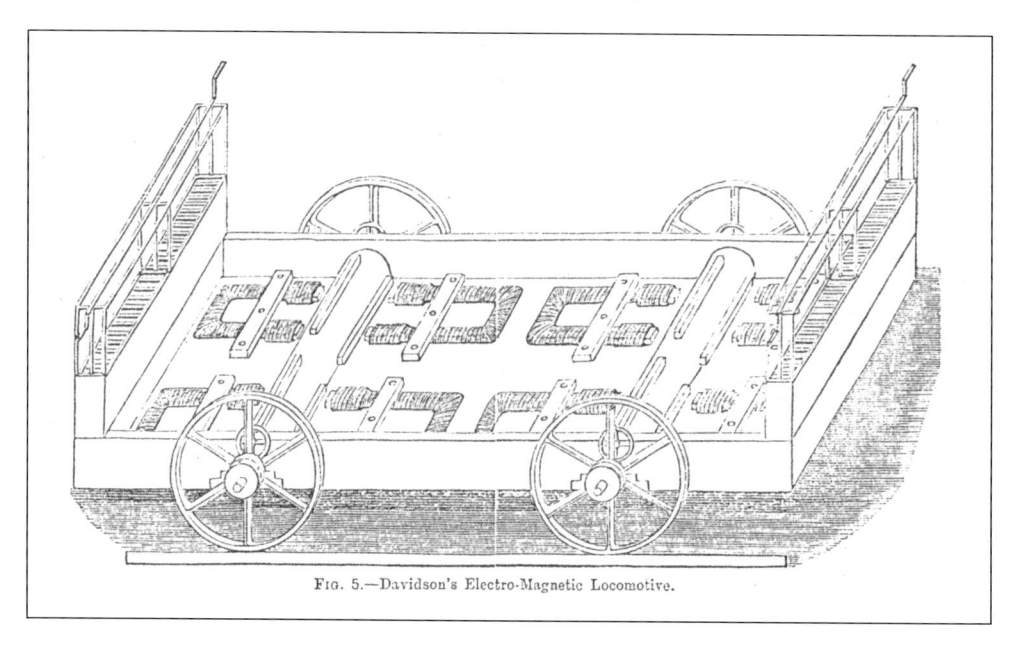

FIG. 5.—Davidson's Electro-Magnetic Locomotive.

Mackie specifically names this as being Davidson's locomotive and in consequence this drawing has always been used in the subsequent, rather rare, historian's descriptions of the machines, as a picture of the locomotive. But there is another drawing, made either by Davidson or at least under his supervision, which shows a much more credible version of the locomotive. It now seem likely that the drawing by Mackie is not of the locomotive that trundled along the railway line between Edinburgh and Glasgow, but rather that it is of an earlier machine which the Davidson himself called a "steerable carriage".

Poster, Printed by Electromagnetism!

In early 1843, Robert Davidson staged an exhibition of his inventions at the Egyptian Hall in London and, to publicise it, he had posters printed on a printing press powered by his own electric motor. This poster shows an excellent drawing of a railway carriage and a locomotive that the inventor had named "Galvani" in honour of the discoverer of electricity. This representation of the carriage matches exactly what is known of the first class carriages of the Edinburgh and Glasgow Railway on whose railroad the locomotive had been demonstrated, so it must be assumed that the engine too is equally accurately drawn. There is also a compelling technical reason why this must be the true picture of the locomotive. In this version it can be seen that the wheels are indirectly driven by chain instead of being attached directly to the motor shafts as in the earlier picture. Extensive tests on the motors have shown that this is the only practical way in which the locomotive could have been driven.

There is much greater certainty about the motors themselves. Mackie has left us a very good drawing of the motor that powered the printing press and which, in a modified form, could have been fitted equally well into the locomotive. A model is shown overleaf. The figure of the man gives an idea of the size of the motor. It has a flywheel five feet in diameter. It has been possible to carry out an extensive series of electrical tests on this model and to build up, qualitatively, a good indication of the electrical characteristics of the full-size Davidson motor.

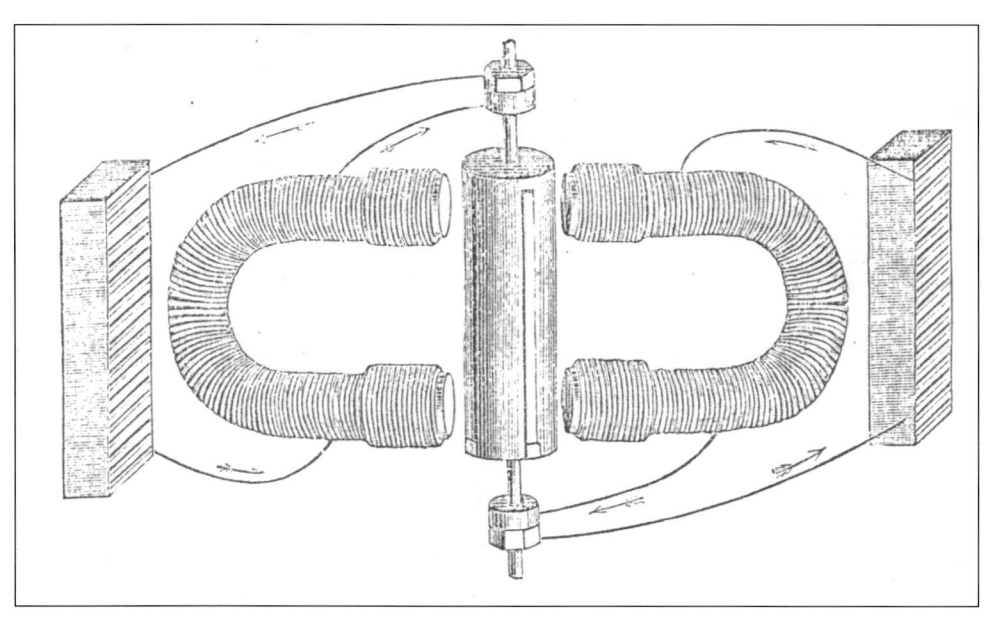

The diagramatic illustration of the motor, provided by Dr Mackie, shows how it worked. It would, today, be described as self-switched reluctance motor, but according to Mackie it worked "by the destruction of magnetism". When compared with other contemporary attempts at electric motors, it was both mechanically and electrically simple. Its mechanical design was more in line with the motors built half a century later. The armatures, with bearings at either end, were wooden cylinders with three equally spaced iron bars lying along their periphery. On opposite sides of the armature was fixed a electromagnet. Each magnet was connected through a rotary switch or commutator attached to the motor shaft, to a voltaic battery consisting of plates of iron and zinc, immersed in sulphuric acid. As the armature rotated and as one of the iron bars was approaching the poles of one of the magnets, the switch contacts for that magnet were closed for a short period, energising it momentarily and so giving an additional turning force to the armature. Because there were three bars and two pairs of magnets, when the current was switched off from the first magnet there would then be a bar approaching the poles of the magnet on the other side. That would then be energised, attracting the bar and giving further rotation to the armature and so on.

There was one serious fault in this arrangement. As the armature bar approached the centre line of the magnets, the force acting on it became more and more perpendicular to the axis of the armature; contributing less and less to the turning force but at the same time adding an increasing heavy frictional load on the bearings. With hind sight, we can see that had Davidson used an even number of bars on his armature and made a small change to the switches, he could have balanced out these undesirable forces and considerably improved his motors. Nevertheless, the motors of this unknown Scotsman were still well in advance of any of his contemporaries.

There is another interesting characteristic of the motors. The windings of the magnets are highly inductive electric circuits, and as the switches break the current flowing through them, a high voltage is induced. This results in a powerful spark at the switch contacts. Contemporary reports of Davidson's locomotive graphically describe it as proceeding along the track making a veritable firework display of sparks. It is likely that Davidson welcomed the publicity value of this striking feature, but we know now that, not only did it diminish the efficiency of the motors, it must have played havoc with the contacts. In the model, a little modern technology – the fitting of quenching diodes – has cured this fault and the motors run smoothly and quietly.

According to the few records available, Davidson's locomotive was about 16 feet long and 6 feet wide; reports of its weight vary from four to six tons. These dimensions would seem to match the size of other rolling stock on the Edinburgh and Glasgow Railway. At either end were compartments for the batteries; the two motors were fitted in between them, their armatures reaching from one side of the vehicle to the other. Instead of a single horseshoe electromagnet on either side of the armature, Davidson fitted two magnets placed side by side, making four in number for each motor. To reduce weight, the cores of the magnets were hollow, built up of ordinary iron sheets. It is very unlikely that any special iron was used and so the weight saving was obtained at the expense of efficiency. The use of "Swedish iron" for magnetic purposes had yet to come. The windings were probably of copper wire, insulated with cotton thread. This sort of wire will be associated, in the minds of some older readers, with the early days of radio, but it was, in fact, available two hundred years earlier. Davidson could well have obtained it from his wife's dress-maker who would have used it to make the framework of the elaborate dresses of that period.

The picture on the Exhibition poster shows that the two motors together drove a single pair of wheels of the locomotive; not both pairs as Mackie's drawing would suggest. This is a most important feature. If the motors were directly attached to the wheels as he shows them, then, at a top speed of 4mph, the armatures would be only turning at the very low speed of about 40rpm. Tests on the models showed that Davidson's motors were, inherently, inefficient at low speeds such as this. However, with a chain drive as shown in the picture, and by using a small sprocket wheel on the armatures and a much larger one on the wheels, it would have been possible to increase the relative speeds by some four to six times, with a corresponding increase of motor efficiency. There was another advantage of this arrangement. Because the current had to be switched on for a series of relatively short periods during each revolution of the armature, there were a number of positions of the armature where no current passed. If the machine had happened to stop with both armatures at one of these positions, then it would not start again until one or other had been moved into an active position. With the armatures coupled together through the chain and sprocket wheel, it was possible to synchronise the two armatures in such a way that the dead spots never occurred together.

During the testing of the models, it immediately became apparent that the angular positions of the armature, relative to the poles of the electromagnets, when the current was switched on and off, were very critical indeed. Another feature was also manifest. If this position was altered beyond a certain point, the motor commenced to rotate in the opposite direction. It is quite inconceivable that Davidson, when testing his machines, would not have been well aware of these features. In the model locomotive, a simple lever has been fitted which allows the switch contacts to be moved between the forward and reverse running positions. Although there is no definite evidence that a similar arrangement was fitted to the locomotive Galvani, it would be doing Davidson an injustice not to credit him with the recognition of the value of such a simple device. The ability to reverse the direction of a vehicle is surely so important that he must have taken advantage of this characteristic of his motors.

The motors occupied approximately seven eighths of the space available, leaving only one eighth for the battery. This relatively small volume emphasises yet another aspect of Davidson's achievement, the nature of the batteries themselves. It was apparent, even before the model was built, that the amount of energy likely to be available from a battery such as Mackie described, was woefully inadequate. How did he get his machine to make the one and a quarter of a mile journey?

The battery compartments at either end of the vehicle consisted of twenty deep wooden boxes each containing, according to Mackie, a sheet of zinc sandwitched between two iron plates, approximately 12 by 8 inches. Each wooden box was partly filled with dilute sulphuric acid. By means of ropes and a lifting handle, the plates could all, simultaneously, be raised or lowered into the pockets of acid below them. The iron and zinc plates, connected in series, were attached by loose cables to the separate motors; when the plates were lowered into the acid a voltage was generated causing the motors to turn.

Zinc and iron electrodes, in dilute sulphuric acid constitute a voltaic cell, but by modern standards a very inefficient one. It produces a voltage of the order of half a volt and the current it is able to generate is small. It was difficult to believe that such a simple battery could ever produce sufficient energy to power a five ton locomotive. When Davidson made his first trial run, he found it necessary to add a further 19 cells to the 40 already there, but the impression is that eventually he was able to make do with only the 40. When the model was built; the motors ran well if connected to ordinary dry cells but the small iron – zinc cells were totally inadequate.

In 1840, the idea of alchemistry was still not far removed from the ordinary person's mind and secret nostrums that worked wonders were a familiar part of the doctor's medicine bag. Did Davidson, with his knowledge of chemistry find some secret ingredient that he could add to the battery to give him enhanced performance. It is on record that Davidson did invent an improved battery but no details can be found today. One simple addition that he might have tried was potassium bichromate. A small quantity of this substance added to the sulphuric acid of the model cells increased their output threefold – but it was still nothing like enough to do the work required of them.

With systems as complex as this, it is very difficult to transpose quantities over a scale of one to twelve with any confidence. So it was decided to make a single full size cell and to see what it would do. Like its small scale counterpart, its open circuit voltage was 0.49 volts. This dropped to 0.44 volts when a current of 7.8 amps was taken from the cell. Even with the 59 cells used in the first trials, Davidson would only have had some 200 watts to drive the machine – enough, perhaps, to drive a vacuum cleaner but hardly a five ton locomotive. The addition of potassium bichromate, as with the small cells, gave a noticeable improvement but this was not sufficient, it would seem, to power the full size engine.

In 1840, the electric battery was in its infancy, the dry cell and the storage battery had yet to come. Many inventors were developing new types of electric cells but they all had complications such as requiring porous vessels and two separate fluids. However, at just about this time, a German, Wilhelm Bunsen, invented a new cell that we now know as the Bichromate cell. It had several similarities to the one that Davidson had arranged for his locomotive. Like his, the electrodes were suspended above the electrolyte until the cell was put to use. The liquid was sulphuric acid, to which, Bunsen had added either chromic acid or potassium bichromate. The principal difference was that the iron plates were changed to carbon.

Full size Zinc–Iron cell.

Did Davidson, perhaps through his friends in the University, get to hear of this new cell? Or did he himself devise or invent something along these lines? All he needed to do was to change his iron plates to carbon ones and add some chromic acid to the acid in his cells. The bichromate cell was a vastly more powerful source of electricity than his.

To test the idea, the iron plates of the full-size cell were replaced with carbon ones and chromic acid added to the electrolyte. The effect on the power delivered was dramatic. Instead of half of a volt, the cell provided more than two volts – and that at a current of well over a hundred amps. Over eight kilowatts from the 40 cells would have been available. This was a much more practical possibility of driving the five ton locomotive.

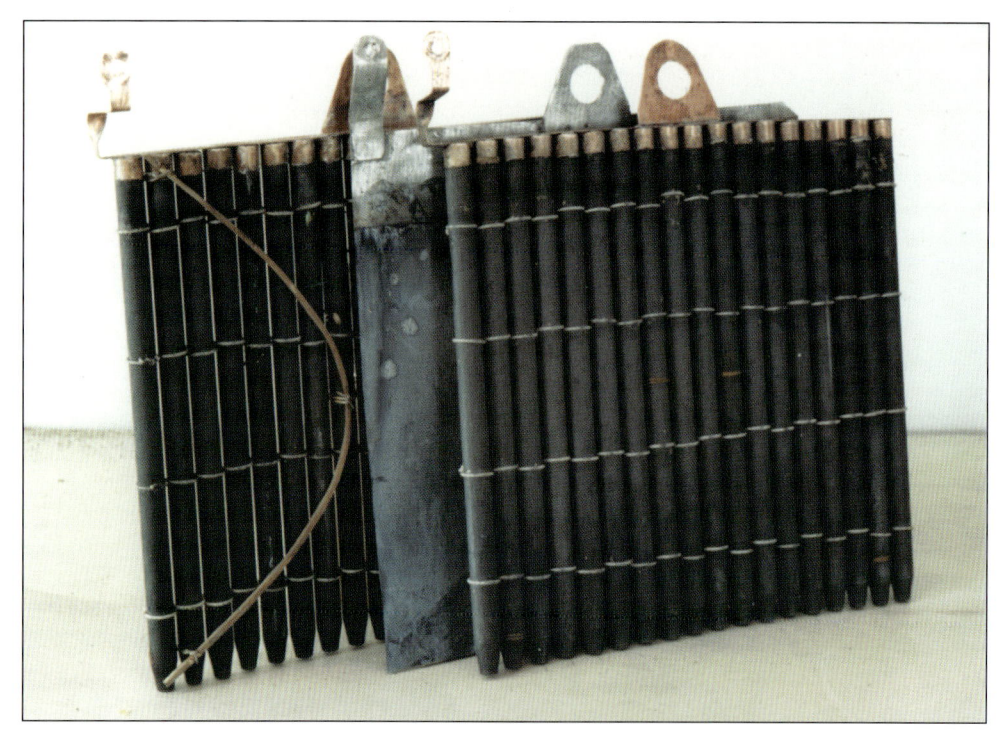

Electrodes of Zinc–Carbon cell. This cell developed 113 amps at 1.59 volts.

Did Davidson know of work going on at the same time as far away as Germany? It seems unlikely? Did he invent something like this himself ? I think that he must have done, and if so, it ranks with some of the most important discoveries in the world of electrical engineering.

Robert Davidson lived to the ripe old age of 95, and at the end of his life he saw – at last – the beginnings of an electric railway being built in London; of a revolution in transport which he had forecast so many years before. I wonder what he must have thought then? He could well have said "I told you so".

He was a shining example of those old time mechanics – a man of simple and honest purpose; blessed with the true spirit of creativity and modest with it all. He did not see his gifts of intuition and of skill as something that he could exploit for his own benefit but as something which he had to pass on to the rest of mankind. We all owe so much to such as he.

Chapter 14

Making the Models

Making models of mechanical devices, particularly of steam powered machines goes back almost to the beginning of mechanical engineering itself, and it is easy to see why. The first steam engines were huge, heavy and even in those days, very expensive, their cost effectiveness was doubtful and indeed many of the first machines were, in one way or another, failures. So smaller and cheaper models of the machines were built, not only to give confidence to the inventor that his brain child would do all that he hoped of it but also to impress and convince his potential customer.

As steam engines became part of the everyday life of the man in the street, another sort of model began to appear. A hundred years ago, steam was the over-riding force which was changing the lives of everyone; steam engines of every sort and shape were proliferating in the factory and on the land and on the sea; but the archetype of steam power was the steam railway locomotive. In the factory and mill, in the ship at sea, steam was the hidden power behind the scene, but on the railway track the wonderful, powerful and indeed, the truly magnificent steam locomotive was revealed in all its glory for all to see. It is small wonder that every young boy wanted to become an engine driver!

Of course, in real life, very few boys grew up to be engine drivers and very few indeed could ever have owned such a wondrous machine; in every way the real thing was well outside their grasp. But it was not so if the engine could be brought down to miniature size – to be made as a toy. So men who were fortunate enough to have the time and money to spare and had not forgotten their childhood dreams, started to build beautiful, miniature steam engines and tiny working models of steam locomotives and so the hobby, indeed the art of model engineering, was born. Some very beautiful examples of the work of these amateur builders can still be seen today.

Model engineering societies were formed – the Society of Model and Experimental Engineers was formed in London in 1898 and others followed suit. Today there are many spread all over the world and many tens of thousands of folk, both men and women, both in and outside the recognised societies, who have found, as I have done, a wonderful hobby.

Model engineering, to many, is still centred on the steam locomotive. To very many, a childhood dream to be an engine driver has become reality even if it is only by putting on an engine driver's cap, sitting astride an incongruously small but very accurate copy of a steam train and trundling round a small railway track. Chacun a son gout. This may be the picture that many people see when they hear of model engineering but it is only the final phase of the hobby, of maybe, many years of dedicated, absorbing, work of building and testing a wonderful piece of precision engineering. Today the steam locomotive is still the centre of attraction of, perhaps,

50% of model engineers, but with the development of modern technology, the range of engineering has broadened dramatically and model engineering has followed suit both in range and nature – and in the methods and techniques available to build the models. Now it includes as subjects, every conceivable mechanical device and it uses equally diverse technology to achieve its ends.

For all its change, however, model making is still primarily concerned with fashioning metal and it still uses the same fundamental, but perhaps somewhat smaller, tools that were used to create the great steam locomotives. Hammer and spanner, drill, chisel, saw and a very wide range of other hand tools are the basic tools of engineering and of model making as well. However, heavy, modern machinery demands, in addition, both the strength and the precision of machine tools. In model making, strength is not so important but precision is essential and so the quintessential of machine tools – the lathe – has become the basic tool of the model maker. Building today's models requires much in addition to cutting metal but nevertheless, a small lathe is perhaps the one essential tool of the model maker.

Although a range of other small power tools has been used in building the models shown here, with the exception of the lathe, none were essential. Indeed, it can be claimed that there is virtue in the use of a great deal of handwork when the subjects that are modelled are early primitive machines. It inevitably leaves signs – signs that must also have been upon the originals, similarly made a hundred or so years before.

Not just iron, but wood, stone and brickwork were equally important materials both in the models and in the prototypes. However, there is one characteristic in which the last three differ from iron; they have a visible structure – a grain. Metal looks exactly the same whether the part from which it is made is at full size or at small scale. This is not so, with wood. Oak was used a great deal in old engineering works but, as for example, in the model of Smeetons Portable Engine tower, a piece of oak an inch wide with the characteristic "figure" of the oak grain showing prominently, just does not "look right". It does not convince the mind that it is supposed to be an oak beam 1 foot wide – the size of the grain is all wrong.

The problem of making structured materials look realistic at a greatly reduced scale inevitably involves some degree of faking. Again, the model of Smeeton's wooden tower is an example. The original tower was almost certainly made of oak; so was the model. Planed and varnished, it looked all wrong, so it was scoured as hard as possible with a rotating wire brush, a trace of grey print was rubbed in and then it was dull varnished. The result; still unmistakably oak, but apparently deeply weathered as was to be expected of a structure of this sort.

With Trevithick's Carriage, a different solution was found. The woodwork of a gentleman's carriage could not be depicted as weathered! In this case, a misfortune turned out to have a happy ending. A lovely strawberry tree (arbutis uneedo) in my garden blew down in a gale and, when I examined this unusual wood I found it to be hard, brown in colour and with occasional tiny knots about a tenth of an inch in diameter. One or two of these in selected positions gave just the exact appearance of wood at the right scale. Surely, the uprooting of my old tree was a good example of serendipity. However, strawberry tree wood is not likely to be available to many model makers, and usually the best way of dealing with wood is to select one with a